KT-594-367

Michael Collins

Pope Benedict XVI

SUCCESSOR TO PETER

the columba press

First published in 2005 by
the columba press
55a Spruce Avenue, Stillorgan Industrial Park, Blackrock, Co
Dublin

Designed by Bill Bolger
Cover photograph © Getty Images
Origination by The Columba Press
Printed in Ireland by
Betaprint, Dublin

ISBN 1 85607 503 6

4528286

ST. MARY'S ROAD
BRANCH

Copyright © 2005, Michael Collins

Contents

Author's Note

As the pontificate of Pope John Paul II drew to a close, Catholics were not alone in wondering who the next Pope might be. The Polish pontiff had made enormous strides in more than a quarter of a century as the Successor of Peter. As he criss-crossed the globe, he had literally put the church on every agenda. But there were critical voices who were worried about the direction in which the church was going. After a highly visible and vocal pontificate, some feared that the papacy was over-identified with Karol Wojtyla. The election of Joseph Ratzinger seemed an antidote. His life had been quite modest by comparison. But there has been huge interest generated in the papacy and it is natural that we wish to know something about this 'humble worker in the vineyard of the Lord'. I am grateful to Seán O Boyle of The Columba Press for the invitation to fill in a gap in our knowledge. Cardinal Joseph Ratzinger wrote extensively and gave wide-ranging interviews. This book has been culled mainly from his writings. He is, to my knowledge, the first professional theologian, as we know the term, to become Pope. Whether one agrees with him or not on many issues, nobody can deny that this is a person of enormous cultural and intellectual talents. I hope that this short book will serve as an introduction to the thought and aims of the new Pope as he begins his challenging pontificate.

My thanks to Kathleen and Gerry Noonan for their help with proof-reading.

Michael Collins

CHAPTER ONE

The Early Days

Joseph Ratzinger was born in the small town of Marktl am Inn in southern Germany on 16 April 1927. The little rural town was close to the northern border of Austria. Joseph was the third and last child born to Joseph and Maria. His father was a police officer, although the Ratzingers were of farming stock and traced their ancestors back through several generations in the area.

The infant was baptised on the very day of his birth, which that year fell on Holy Saturday. It was a tradition among the people at that time to have newly born children baptised immediately as the incidence of infant mortality was high. The little boy was taken to the local church where the ceremonies for Holy Saturday had just been celebrated. In those days, the Easter Vigil was carried out on the morning, rather than the evening of Holy Saturday. It was seen as a special blessing in the Ratzinger family that the youngest child had been baptised by the parish priest with newly blessed water.

Any blessings which could be gained were gladly accepted, for those were difficult years. The First World War had ended in a disastrous defeat for the Germans less than a decade earlier, in 1918. A people who had long suffered turmoil and violence were still reeling from the economic straits in which they found themselves after the war.

The Bavarians trace their past with great pride. Among the earliest to settle on their lands were the Celts, who brought a rich folklore and elaborate skill in arts and crafts. In the first century, the Romans occupied the land, offering the people protection and prosperity in exchange for loyalty to Rome. When the Roman Empire collapsed in the West in the late fifth century AD, the area was settled by German tribes who nonetheless managed to forge a harmonious existence with the Roman remnant. In 787, Charlemagne annexed the territories for himself and for three centuries the people were subject to Carolingian rule. By 1180, the Bavarian family dynasty of Wittelsbach took control of the area when Otto VI was nominated Duke of Bavaria by Holy Roman Emperor Frederick I, Barbarossa. During the Reformation, Bavaria remained faithful to the Catholic faith. In 1648, the Treaty of Westphalia reconfirmed the dictum of the Peace of Augsburg, passed in 1555. This set of negotiations had decreed a memorable Latin tag, *cuius rego, eius religio*, whatever the faith of the ruler was to be the faith of the populace. Bavaria was to be at the crossroads of various warring armies throughout the seventeenth to nineteenth centuries, until it finally united itself with the German Empire in 1871. Participating in the First World War, it suffered the humiliating defeat of the rest of Germany.

When Joseph was just under two years old, the Ratzinger family moved from their comfortable lodgings in Marktl am Inn for Tittmoning, a small town close to the border of Austria. Here his father received a new commission in the town. It was a considerable promotion, and the family found itself living in the police barracks in the main square of the town. The house had formerly belonged to a religious order, and although imposing from the outside, it had a rather austere interior. They settled in quickly.

Joseph was quite close in age to his brother, Georg and his sister Maria. While the children enjoyed the freedom to play in the meadows close to the house, trouble was brewing on the horizon.

Following the end of the First World War, Germany had reluctantly accepted the provisions of the Treaty of Versailles. Subsequent political analysts have seen that the terms of punishment were harsh in the extreme, and indeed unjust to the population. As a result, Germans experienced a Great Depression, marked by economic stagnation, unemployment and monetary inflation. Throughout the 1920s, a young political activist, Adolf Hitler, agitated for action to help Germany emerge from its woes. As part of his plan, Hitler advocated widening the German territories to allow greater *lebensraum*, or living space, for the native people. Following the Wall Street Crash of 1929, some German entrepreneurs began to look more favourably on Hitler's political activities, convinced that he could provide a cohesive way out of the political crisis.

As a police officer, Joseph's father found himself in opposition to the increasingly fanatical 'brownshirts', or supporters of Hitler. The young children did not understand what was happening at the time, but they realised that it was a period of intense anxiety for their parents. It was a considerable relief to the family when Ratzinger senior received a new post towards the end of 1932. Shortly before Christmas, the Ratzingers said farewell to their neighbours in Tittmoning and set off for the prosperous town of Aschau am Inn at the foot of the Alps. The family could scarcely believe their good luck. The living quarters had been rented from a farmer who had recently built a fine house in the country. There was a large garden and in a nearby meadow, a carp pond. Joseph Ratzinger learned to respect water there, because while playing beside it he almost fell in and drowned.

The accommodation was on the second floor, directly

above the station. It was somewhat more rural than Tittmoning, but the family settled in quickly. For Joseph's father, the political situation continued to cause concern. Just over a month after their arrival, President Hindenburg transferred power to Adolf Hitler. The Nazi party which he led won a majority in the election. A year later, Hitler became Chancellor. On 27 February 1933, the German parliament building, the Reichstag, was destroyed by fire. The following day, Hitler, on the pretext of preventing a Communist takeover, forced President Hindenburg to sign a decree proclaiming a state of emergency. Less than a month later, with further election victories in favour of the Nazis, Hitler received plenipotentiary powers from the newly-elected parliament.

Even though Bavaria was far-removed from the frenetic political storm in the north, slowly the 'seizure of power' seeped southwards to the region. In his memoirs, *Milestones*, Joseph Ratzinger recalled how both the covert and open Nazi sympathisers brought their brown shirts out of the trunk. 'The "Hitler Youth" and "League of German Girls" were introduced, and my brother and sister were obliged to participate in their activities.' (*Milestones*, p 15) Joseph's father was horrified by what he saw, and tried to maintain some semblance of calm in face of the escalating storm. Joseph, along with his class, was also enlisted in the Hitler Youth movement in 1943, although he did not attend their meetings. As the son of the local policeman, there was no possibility of avoiding the movement which had by now become compulsory.

All about there were 'enemies of the Reich', and neighbours informed upon each other for failure to embrace the Nazi party enthusiastically. The priests, in particular, became prime targets for their intransigence in the face of the Nazi progress. In 1933 Hitler had signed a Concordat with the Vatican, in which he promised to honour the rights of Catholics, but he immediately repudiated his contract. The Concordat was signed in Munich by the papal nuncio, Eugenio Pacelli, the future Pope Pius XII. One of the key issues was church and state education. In Bavaria, there was a solid link between school and parish. Often the local schoolmaster was also organist and choir-director. Hitler realised that such a situation would not foster the type of youth he wanted. The young Joseph recalled in later life how letters from the bishops were read from the pulpit of his local church. In these pastoral letters, the bishops denounced the duplicitous Chancellor and his repudiation of the Concordat. Joseph was puzzled by the tone of the episcopal letters, which demanded that the status quo should be preserved at all costs. He displayed precocious powers of criticism during these four years when he observed that 'empty institutions' were bound to failure.

Encouraged by the national success of the Nazis, new ideas began to infiltrate the small town of Aschau. In leter years Ratzinger recalled how a gifted young teacher erected a Maypole to banish the superstition of Christianity and re-establish the wise ideals of the Teutonic race. 'But in those days, such rhetorical formulas hardly impressed the sober mentality of Bavarian farmers. The young men were more interested in the sausages which hung from the Maypole (which were grabbed by the fastest climbers) than in the high-flown phrases of the schoolteacher.' (*Milestones*, p 16)

The young children's education had to be attended to, and the senior Ratzingers selected carefully the schools which their children would attend. Joseph displayed an interest in learning from a young age, as well as a love for music. In 1935, his brother Georg entered the gymnasium, or classical school in nearby Traunstein. In that same year, Joseph entered the school at the Franciscan convent of Au am Inn.

The boys became altar-servers, and attended the regular Masses and processions which marked life in the village.

The Ratzingers brought their children to the religious services and explained to them the meaning of the liturgy which they attended. One of Joseph's most prized possessions was a missal, with pictures alongside the prayers. To this day, it is still common to give German children these illustrated missals which help them understand the liturgy. In those days, the Mass was celebrated in Latin. Joseph had begun to learn Latin in school and was soon enamoured of its poetic cadences. Above all, this introduced him to the world of the liturgy, where he felt heaven and earth touched. It marked the beginning of a life-long fascination with the liturgy and its treasures.

Change was to intrude once more into the Ratzinger family, but this time it was most welcome. Police officers retired at the relatively young age of sixty, a concession to their often-demanding duties. After a period of extended sick leave, Joseph's father retired from the service on 6 March 1937. In view of the deteriorating political situation, this was not a day too early for him. In preparation for retirement, Joseph's parents had bought a farmhouse on the edge of Traunstein. It was a village of some 11,500 people. Although not quite as comfortable as their former residence, it had the advantage of being nearer school for the boys, less than half an hour's walk.

For the children, the rickety house was their closest experience to paradise. Set in a large meadow, the house was built of wood, in the familiar Alpine style. On one side of the house was an oak grove and on the other a large pine forest. In the front garden were two cherry blossoms and a well. Since the house did not have running water, trips were undertaken regularly to fill the basins for washing and household chores. Iron stoves provided heating in the cold winters, and during the hot summers the breezes from the mountains were welcome.

At the local school, young Joseph learned Greek and Latin as well as his native German. There were classes in history, geography, mathematics, religion and music. Already new song books had been prepared for the children by Nazi propagandists. One of the teachers substituted the phrases *Juda den Tod*, 'death to Judah', with *wende die Not*, 'banish our plight'. Within a year of the youngest Ratzinger's arrival, a new form of education was introduced, the *oberschule*. Greek was abandoned and Latin greatly diminished. In compensation, there was greater emphasis on English and the sciences. A few years later, the study of religion was prohibited in school, its place taken by physical exercise. An exception was made for those, like Joseph, who had commenced their religious classes prior to the new rule. It was presumed that study of religion would die out of its own accord.

The children enjoyed the freedom afforded by their new home. Since it was so near the Austrian border, Frau Ratzinger often brought her children to Salzburg, the home of Mozart, to hear the concerts and the orchestral Masses in some of the city churches. On one occasion, they listened enraptured to the famous Regensburg Domspatzen, the cathedral choir. How could young Georg imagine that one day he would conduct the internationally renowned choir?

The children were aware of the rumblings caused by soldiers as they carried out menacing drills. Often Georg and Joseph listened to their father and his friends as they quietly and anxiously discussed the impending hostilities around the kitchen table. On the night of 9 November 1938, the Nazis organised a brutal assault on the homes and workplaces of Jews in Germany. In the Ratzingers' own village of Traunstein, the homes of the few Jews living in the village were attacked. It was the prelude to the horrors that were to come.

CHAPTER TWO

The Second World War

Finally, the clouds of war broke in September 1939, when Joseph was eleven. Already, some months earlier, Czechoslovakia had been occupied. On 1 September 1939, German troops invaded Austria and 'annexed' it to the German state. Austria was to be swallowed up in 'Greater Germany'.

It was about this time that the local pastor asked to see Joseph. Noting the youth's serious demeanour in church, the pastor asked him if he had ever considered becoming a priest. Joseph said that the idea had occurred to him when he was younger but that he had not thought about it recently. The pastor suggested that if he wished, he would make inquiries about joining the local seminary in Freising. This was a school where children received their education in a specifically semi-monastic atmosphere, similar to today's boarding-schools. Already his brother Georg had enrolled in the seminary. But the thought of having two sons in the seminary caused the boys' father to worry. His pension was not very large, and he feared that he could not be expected to pay the term fees. There were no scholarships available. At that time, however, Maria Ratzinger graduated from college and found a job with a company in Traunstein. She was in a position to contribute to the family finances and insisted that if Joseph wished, he could go to the seminary. Knowing that it would provide a good education, no matter what Joseph's final decision would be, the family decided to opt for the seminary.

The young boy was happy there, although his companions later remembered him as a shy and timid youth. He had no interest in sport and even less in some of the practical jokes that the others enjoyed playing. He was serious and was usually found either in the chapel or in the library.

With the outbreak of the war, the seminary was turned into a military hospital to care for the inevitable casualties. Like all Germans of the time, even those against the war, the hope was that hostilities would soon cease. But Hitler made a number of rapid triumphs as German forces swept through Denmark and Norway. Soon Holland, Belgium, Luxemburg and France folded before the Teutonic onslaught. The Balkans were the next victims before Hitler launched his attack on the Soviet Union. With the rapidly deteriorating situation, the seminarians were sent home. When Georg turned seventeen, he was drafted into the army. In the summer of 1942, George was forced to work in the *Reichsarbeitsdienst*, a service of the Reich. As a signal man he saw action in France, Holland, Czechoslovakia and Italy.

The war began to go badly for Germany as more and more serious setbacks were inflicted on it. Thousands upon thousands of soldiers died on the battle fields. The Nazi authorities were forced to use younger and younger children to shore up their rapidly dwindling human resources. In 1943, at the age of sixteen Joseph was drafted, along with other seminarians, into the 'flak' anti-aircraft batteries. Their first mission was to Ludwigsfeld, to the north of Munich. They were given the task of defending the Bavarian Motor Works, which produced motors for planes used in the air force. From there they were transferred to Unterföhring, hence to Innsbruck and finally to Gilching, north of Lake Ammer. Joseph was assigned to a non-combative telecommunications task. The propaganda machine tried to ensure that all the young charges thought that the war was going in Germany's favour. However, the students realised that the war was going badly and worried if they would ever see a victory, or at least a peace established.

For the young Joseph, like most Germans, there was a strong mixture of emotions. His country was at war, and even though he did not agree with the motive, he still felt national pride. Moreover, Germany had now made powerful enemies, and it was by no means certain that, if victorious, they would prove generous with the natives who had precipitated the worst war in recent history. He tried to ignore what was happening around him. But it was impossible. He learned about the concentration camp of Dachau while he was working at the BMW plant. Later, while working with tank traps, he saw Hungarian Jews being moved like cattle in trains. Rumours circulated that they were being shipped to certain death. It was impossible not to be moved by the plight of these victims of Nazi arrogance. He was a young man trying desperately not to believe what was happening all about him. As a cardinal, Joseph was openly critical of the Catholic Church in Germany. The bishops had sought too quickly a *modus vivendi* with Hitler. Without the complacency of some sections of Catholic Germany, the war would not have progressed as far as it did. Pope Pius XII was later to come in for strong criticism for not condemning the atrocities more vocally than he had.

In September 1944, the youths were discharged from the 'flak'. He was proud that he had not borne firearms, as he had suffered a badly infected finger which prevented him taking part in drills. But there was to be no respite. As soon as Joseph arrived home to his parents he found the conscription notice had already been delivered. Within a few days he had to depart once more for the war, this time to Burgenland, close to the border where Austria, Czechoslovakia and Hungary meet. This was a period of utter misery for Joseph. But a month later, in October, Hungary surrendered to Russia. The young man began to realise that Germany's fate was sealed. In November he and his comrades were ordered to leave Burgenland. Their civilian clothes were given back and they boarded trains to bring them home. As he passed through Salzburg, he saw the old city had been badly damaged by the bombs. The cathedral where he had wandered as a child listening to the cadences of the Latin Mass had been directly hit. The great cupola had collapsed.

Arriving home, Joseph's parents were overjoyed. He was noticeably thinner, but had sustained no wounds. He was alive, and that was all they cared about. But the respite was brief, for a month later Joseph was summoned once more to the war effort. Called to Munich, Joseph and his comrades were assigned to posts in the army. The young Ratzinger could scarcely believe his luck when he was appointed to Traunstein. Little did he know that the desperate Nazi authorities had taken to assigning soldiers to their native towns, to dissuade them from deserting. Joseph was unable to perform military duties as a result of ill health. But there was an air of despair. By the time Hitler committed suicide, most Germans had realised that it was only a matter of time before the Americans would cross the borders and enter Germany.

In the spring of 1945, Joseph decided to desert. He plucked up the courage and left by a back road leading out of Traunstein. But when he crossed a railroad underpass, he was stopped by two soldiers. Deserters were to be shot on sight. The young Ratzinger froze with fear of the soldiers. But seeing that he had a wounded arm, they let him pass. He could scarcely believe his good luck and hurried home. The army was disintegrating. Two SS men billeted themselves with the Ratzingers, insisting that the former police officer offer them hospitality. Joseph was terrified that they would realise that he had deserted. But they left after a few days, knowing that the Americans were advancing. However, before they departed, sixty-two remaining prisoners were shot, for the deserting Nazis did not want to leave any prisoners. Finally, the Allied soldiers arrived. They immediately made the Ratzingers' their headquarters in the village. Georg had still not returned from Italy and Joseph was recognised as a soldier. Dressed in his uniform, he was forced to join a procession of prisoners of war who were marched to a camp to face punishment for their war-crimes.

After three days of enforced march, the band arrived at the military airport of Bad Aibling. But the respite was brief and after a few days Joseph was transferred to farmlands on the outskirts of Ulm. Here the Americans rounded up their prisoners of war until they received instructions about their fate. Rations were kept to a minimum: a ladle of soup and some bread was the staple daily diet. Each day, Joseph set his gaze on the majestic contours of Ulm's Gothic cathedral, praying to God for deliverance from the traumatic condition he now found himself in. Some priests, who had served as army chaplains, celebrated Mass on makeshift altars. As the winter turned into spring, there seemed little hope that they would be released. Finally, in early June, the Allied forces decided that there was little danger that the German military remnant would be able to stage a revival. Soldiers who had come from farming stock were the first to be released, so that they could return to the land. It was not until 19 June 1945 that the young Ratzinger was freed and made the 120 mile journey home on the back of a milk van.

Arriving home, he heard singing coming from the village church. Not wanting to interrupt the service, he made for home, where he had a tearful reunion with his father. Soon his mother and sister returned from church, advised by their excited neighbours that young Joseph had been seen dismounting from a milkvan in the square. For Joseph, the joy was by no means complete, as no word had been heard from Georg in several months. The last they had heard was that he had been posted to Italy and the fear was that he had died in the bombing.

It is not difficult the image the joy in the Ratzinger household when, one July day, Georg appeared at the kitchen door. He had not only survived, but managed to make his way home. Now the family was united again, and all the tragedy of the past few years melted into a combination of delight and hope.

In the months following the war, Germans learned piece-meal the full horrors of what had been done in their name. For the young Joseph and Georg, they were deeply troubled by the fact that the war had been fought in the heartland of Christian Europe. This was strongly to influence the development of Joseph's though in the years to come.

CHAPTER THREE

The Seminary

As soon as the war was over, the bishop of the diocese gave orders to open the seminary at Freising. Many of the former seminarians who had been drafted for service had fallen during the war. The old seminary buildings, which had been used as a military hospital for six years, were vacated. The students set to work painting the walls and repairing the shutters on the windows. With the end of the war, the Allies were determined not to make the same mistakes as had been made following the First World War. Germany was to be given reasonable funds, according to the Marshall Plan, to rebuild its economy which lay in ruins. But, funds for repairing and restoring this particular building and other ecclesiastical properties were lacking. Only the determination of the young survivors could ensure that the seminary would reopen and priests be ordained for the diocese. By Christmas 1945, over 120 seminarians had enrolled to train as priests. Several of the seminarians were former soldiers. To the 19-year-old Joseph Ratzinger, these students, many of them in their 40s, were experienced beyond their years. They had come from the length and breadth of Germany

In the aftermath of the war, the seminary, and its reconstruction, gave the students a focus. It was something of which they could be proud. For the young Joseph, this was also his introduction to the world of philosophy and theology. Despite the paucity of the library, there was ample material for the students to read. With the rigour and dedication which is a mark of German scholarship, Joseph began to read the works of several philosophers and theologians. He did not like listening to the radio in the community room, and was to be found in a corner of the building or in his room avidly reading novels which had been denied to him during the six war years. He read von Le Fort, Langgässer, Claudel, Bernanos, Dostoevsky and Mauriac. He was fascinated in particular by the works of Kant, Husserl, Heidegger, Nietzsche, Fichte, as well as Guardini, Pieper and Wust. He found in these writers the stimulation which he craved; St Thomas Aquinas, avidly proposed by the seminary authorities, he found rather dry and removed from real life. Much as he enjoyed his philosophy courses, these were for Joseph only preliminary to his real passion: theology.

There was also time to improve his piano playing, which he had been forced to abandon for the period of the war. Several of his comrades played instruments such as the cello, violin, recorder, flute and trumpet. Once a week they had a period of common recreation at which they staged impromptu concerts, which served to strengthen the spirit of camaraderie. Letters were written to his parents and sister every two weeks. They radiated happiness and a developing spirit of confidence, and during the holiday periods he was able to spend time with his family in their home at Hufschlag, just outside Traunstein.

By the end of 1947, Joseph had completed his two-year philosophy course. He was determined to continue his formation for the priesthood and wrote to the bishop asking for admission to study theology. There were several options open to him. He could opt for the strict seminary at Eichstätt or one of five seminaries which sent their students to Munich State University for their theological studies. Having considered carefully the variety of choices,

Joseph opted for the Herzogliches Georgianum which had been founded in 1494 in Ingolstadt by Duke George the Rich. It was a venerable institution, and for almost five centuries had provided education for students studying for the priesthood in Bavaria. The bishop gave his permission to Joseph and two other students to study at the Georgianum. The standard was high, but that was precisely why Joseph chose it. Already he had decided to embrace theology as a profession.

To the present-day reader, it may be surprising to know that the twenty-one-year-old Joseph Ratzinger had chosen the field of theology with the intention of teaching it. But in previous years, it was not unknown for students for the priesthood to shape their destiny even before ordination. Those with an interest in the diplomatic life had one path open to them. For those interested in teaching, that was also a possibility. Given that the priests received the highest degree of education, it was not uncommon for priests to teach philosophy, theology, music, history or even the sciences, removed entirely from a pastoral setting.

Since the University of Munich lay largely in ruins, it was not possible for the seminarians to study there. Accordingly, the theology faculty had found temporary lodgings in a former royal hunting lodge at Fürstenried. The diocese of Munich had acquired the building after the First World War and established it as a retreat house. It was small and uncomfortable. Joseph was dismayed in his early weeks at how decrepit the building had become and at the poor standard of food. By way of consolation, the nearby castle, which had once belonged to King Ludwig the Mad, had offered the seminarians the use of its grounds. It was to be a welcome refuge for Joseph, who enjoyed wandering its gravel paths under the ancient boughs, thinking of all that he had read and studied.

It was in the greenhouse of the castle garden that lectures were held, as the lodge had no adequate room. In winter, the students wrapped themselves up in every stitch of clothing they had, carefully insulating the warped glass-frames with old newspapers. In summer, the windows were thrown open, the breeze welcome as the temperatures rose in the glass house. It was a rather strange location, but few complained. The lectures were engrossing. The students had a sense of history. In 1938, the Munich Theological Faculty had been suppressed by the Nazis. When the war finally came to an end, the university authorities sought to reconstitute the faculty. However, several members were either dead, or unable to teach. Therefore, the university canvassed outside the region, offering positions to professors on the former faculties of Breslau in Silesia and Braunsberg in Eastern Prussia. Both were renowned faculties, and the students were more than pleased with the new lecturers. In time, the Munich faculty was to develop into a respected source of theology. Among the new staff were Michael Schmaus, who wrote a successful dogmatic textbook in a modern style. It became a highly influential book, presenting dogmatic studies in a clear and concise way for generations of seminarians. Friedrich Wilhelm Maier was the professor of New Testament. He also gained a reputation as a brilliant scholar. It was Maier who made popular the 'two source' theory, which is now accepted almost universally. This taught that Mark was the first gospel to be composed, rather than Matthew, who had been credited as the author of the first gospel for eighteen centuries. He also proposed that a Q source (from the German *Quelle* for source) was the most primitive collection for the sayings of Jesus. Although this source is presumed lost, it provided the earliest written texts for the gospels.

The writings of Protestant scholars were studied with

surprising openness for the period. Barth, Bultmann, and others made enormous contributions to Christian theology in Germany and indeed to the world. The Catholic seminarians read them initially as texts of 'separated brethren' but soon recognised their outstanding scholarship.

Joseph had always a deep love for liturgy and it was books on the development of worship which he most readily devoured. Among these were the works of Odo Casel, a German Benedictine monk who was to have a lifelong influence on Ratzinger. In the Catholic world, the liturgical movement had been growing apace. The war had prevented the young Joseph Ratzinger from travelling, and so he relied on books for his knowledge of other liturgical practices. However, he read with great interest the work of the liturgical writers and developed a deep understanding of the subject. It was to remain a *leitmotif* and passion right into his pontificate. At his Mass to mark the beginning of his pontificate, he insisted that the rite be called the Mass at the Beginning of the Petrine Ministry of the Bishop of Rome.

By late 1949, the situation in Munich had improved to such an extent that the students could return to the old buildings on Ludwigstraße. From there it was a short walk to the university. But for the graduation class, time was running out, and preparations would soon be underway for priestly ordination. The last year was a marvellous experience, but the pressure was on to conclude the studies.

When the final exams were over in the early summer of 1950, Joseph Ratzinger entered a competition. Although there was a small sum of money attached, the real attraction was that if accepted, the work submitted was considered as a dissertation. The way was then opened to a doctorate. This was exactly what Joseph wanted. The theme of the work was announced: 'The People and the

House of God in Augustine's Doctrine of the Church'. The topic could not have been more favourable. Since his earliest encounter with the fifth-century African bishop's writings, Joseph had been captivated by Augustine's thought. He threw himself into the task with his customary zeal. Already as an 18-year-old he had read the *Confessions* in their original Latin. Now he worked his way through the surviving sermons to develop his thesis. It was to occupy him for nine months, throughout the final year of his training for the priesthood.

In October of 1950, Joseph received ordination to the diaconate, an important stepping stone to the priesthood. The final months of training were given over to 'pastoral practice'. This was always kept until shortly before ordination. It was reckoned that only those students with a vocation would have remained at this stage. During these weeks, the candidates for priesthood practiced the elaborate movements of the Latin Mass, the central act of worship in the Catholic liturgy. They would learn how to anoint the sick and dying, blessing them on their hands, feet and head with scented holy oil. The sacrament of penance also required a formula, as did baptisms marriages and the other rituals.

An so, on a warm summer day, on 29 June, the Solemnity of St Peter and St Paul, Joseph Ratzinger found himself standing in the cathedral of Freising. As his name was called, he answered *'Adsum'*, I am here. In his memoirs, the future Pope recalled how, at the very moment the archbishop laid his hands on him, a little bird – perhaps a lark – flew up from the High Altar in the cathedral and trilled a brief joyful song. It was to strike him on many occasions that he should sing for joy for the great privilege of being called to be a minister of God's people. Close by was his brother Georg, who was also ordained a priest with him.

On 8 July, the two brothers returned to their village of Hufschlag to celebrate their first Mass in the church of St Oswald. It was a huge affair and the tiny church was packed. The High Altar was alight with candles and covered with summer flowers. The two brothers wore elaborately decorated cloth of gold chasubles, intertwined with vines and sheafs of wheat. Joseph celebrated Mass first, followed by his brother. Concelebration was not restored in the church until after the Second Vatican Council. The choir sang music by Haydn and Mozart. At the end of the Mass, the two brothers stood for three hours giving their first blessing.

CHAPTER FOUR

Into Academia

A pastoral appointment now awaited Joseph. After a short vacation spent with his parents, he took up a position on 1 August in the parish of the Precious Blood in Munich. It was a suburban setting, and he was the assistant pastor. It was much busier than he had expected and he found it difficult to adapt to the change from the sedentary pace of seminary to the bustle of parish. Each day he rose at five o'clock and heard confessions from six until seven. Mass was celebrated at seven thirty each morning, more often than not at a side altar. On Saturdays he spent four hours in the confessional and on Sundays he celebrated at least two Masses. In addition there were baptisms, weddings and funerals to attend. As the newly-arrived assistant pastor, he was put in charge of youth ministry. This proved more difficult than he imagined and his natural shyness made it difficult to relate to the young children. He also had some elementary teaching – some sixteen hours a week. With his penchant for discipline, he prepared the lessons assiduously, but he soon realised that the children had a poor religious education and there was great scope for work. With some relief, he received an assignment to the seminary at Freising, commencing on 1 October 1952. He was to give a series of lectures on pastoral ministry to the final year students.

Initially, the young Fr Ratzinger thought that returning to the seminary would be just what he wanted. Once more he would be able to embrace his theological work, and perhaps forge ahead in carving a career as a theologian. He would be able to press on with his doctorate, which he hoped to finish within the year. But teaching his juniors proved more difficult than he had imagined, and pastoral commitments in the cathedral bit into his time. His greatest satisfaction came in July 1953 when he received his doctorate at the end of his studies. Now the road was open to write his *habilitation*, a volume or thesis which would be accepted by the university to grant him a full-time teaching position.

Fr Ratzinger's career began to move rapidly. At the end of the summer, he received an informal invitation to replace Fr Otfried Müller at the College for Philosophy and Theology in Freising. It was a junior post, but it would be the first step on an important teaching career if he accepted it. The problem was that the offer came too soon. He did not feel confident that he could both teach and write his *habilitation* at the same time. Reluctantly, he turned down the position. But the authorities must have had their eye on the young theologian, for a year later they offered him the post once again. This time he accepted. He had gathered enough information to begin his *habilitation* on the writings of St Bonaventure, the thirteenth century Franciscan theologian.

Another stroke of good fortune came the same year. One of the professors resident at the college had died, thus vacating a house for the next arrival. Joseph Ratzinger now found himself with lodgings which went with the position. This was more than he could have hoped for. But setting up a house required time and money. Instead he opted to teach the required hours and take up temporary lodgings. In the first year he delivered a set of dogmatic lectures on God. These amounted to four hours a week, which required about twelve of preparation. In addition, he began to write up his *habilitation*.

It proved to be a more difficult task than he had imagined. The teaching was taxing, but the research was more arduous than he had anticipated. He began to understand how difficult it is to develop a clear teaching style while also doing good original research. He gave up whatever pastoral duties he had undertaken in order to concentrate on the writing of his *habilitation*. By October 1955, a typewritten copy was ready for submission to the theology faculty in Munich.

Now he could concentrate on the house. The idea of moving into the large residence on his own was not attractive. He considered subletting part of it, but decided that he was probably not sufficiently practical to look after the administration it would require. Finally he decided to put the question to his parents. Would they consider moving in with him? The old house, two miles out of Traunstein, was too big for them also. His father was now seventy-eight and his mother seventy-one. This seemed a solution acceptable to all. His sister Maria also indicated that she would join him shortly.

On 17 November, his parents bid a sad farewell to their home of two decades and set off for Freising. Joseph was surprised at how little furniture they brought with them, but by nightfall the house had been put in order and they sat down to a meal prepared by his mother.

With all the excitement of moving, Joseph had forgotten the *habilitation* which he had submitted some months earlier. His supervisor, Gottlieb Söhngen had assured him that the standard was more than adequate and that it would be a formality for the second reader to approve the work. Michael Schmaus, his old professor in the seminary, was the second reader. Joseph was pleased and since he had a very high regard for Schmaus, he presumed that all would go well.

The months passed and he received no word about his

CORK CITY LIBRARY

work. At Easter the following year, he bumped into Fr Schmaus at a theological congress. He asked his former lecturer if he had read the *habilitation*. Schmaus told him that he had and that he had decided to reject it. This was like a clap of thunder. One of the foremost theologians of the time had rejected his work out of hand. But Schmaus went on. It was, moreover, substandard, poorly written and the thesis was untenable.

Apart from the effect on his ego, there was the question of the house. The accommodation was awarded in connection with the teaching position. With his *habilitation* rejected, it was unlikely that he could still teach. What would happen his parents? Schmaus was determined not to change his mind. However, he did not have the final say. A faculty meeting was convened to decide how to proceed. Despite Schmaus's strong reservations, Joseph Ratzinger was given a chance to revise his work. For the young theologian, this was a true lifeline. From friends connected with the faculty, he learned that he had developed a reputation for being too modern.

Joseph was dismayed but he was determined to re-submit the thesis. Working with extreme rapidity, he succeeded in concluding the rewritten work by October. But once again he had to endure four months of anxiety as he waited a final judgement from the faculty. At last, on 11 February he received a letter. His *habilitation* had been accepted. He was called to give a defence of the work in public on 21 February. Word had spread rapidly about the Ratzinger case. The auditorium where the defence was to take place was packed with excited students. It was possible to fail here, in public, and such events were always followed with great interest. In the event, they were not disappointed. The two official readers engaged in an argument between themselves, which left Joseph Ratzinger somewhat in the background.

After a lengthy debate, the faculty withdrew. It seemed like hours for the anxious Fr Ratzinger, who had to wait with his brother Georg in the corridor. They could hear shouting from the room where the faculty were debating his thesis. One of the agitated voices was that of Michael Schmaus. Finally, the door of the faculty office opened and the dean stepped out. He curtly informed the young priest that his habilitation had been accepted.

With an enormous feeling of relief, he ran home to tell his parents. The path was now clear for his advancement in the world of academia which he had so long desired and for which he had worked. Within a few months he was appointed lecturer at Munich University, and at the beginning of 1958, he received the professorship of fundamental theology and philosophy in Freising. This was to open a new chapter in his life.

CHAPTER FIVE

The Second Vatican Council

On 15 April 1959, Dr Joseph Ratzinger delivered his first lecture as ordinary professor of fundamental theology at the University of Bonn. His time in Freising had been brief. Already an informal invitation had been extended to the young candidate in the summer of the previous year. At the same time Georg had concluded his master's in music and had been appointed to teach music at the seminary in Traunstein. He was also to take over the choir in his home parish of St Oswald, where he had been so recently ordained. Accommodation was provided in Traunstein for the choir director. The two brothers debated the possibility of their parents moving back to Traunstein to be nearer their old home. Georg's house was large and there would be plenty of space for his parents. Eventually they decided to return to Traunstein rather than travel north with Joseph.

Bonn was a highly respected university and the theology faculty was regarded as full of promise in post-war Germany. One of the most prominent lecturers was Theodor Klauser, who founded the influential *Reallexicon für Antike und Christentum*. Also teaching on the staff was Hubert Jedin, the great church historian who had been harboured at the Vatican during the war. At first Joseph found it difficult to adapt to the northern Germans and their temperament. But there was an enormous sense of relief at having achieved his *habilitation* and he embarked on what had been a cherished dream for years.

The intellectual stimulation was all that he had hoped for. Several Bavarian colleagues had also obtained teaching posts in Bonn. The climate of theology was a great deal more open than that taught in Bavaria, which was somewhat insular. The young Ratzinger was fascinated to meet his colleagues who debated issues which he had never heard addressed seriously during his training. In particular he enjoyed speaking with colleagues from the Lutheran traditions and those who had studied world religions.

When he returned to Traunstein in the summer, a personal tragedy awaited him. His father suffered a severe stroke, and after two days in hospital, he died. The small family was fractured and the bereavement hung heavily on them. In his memoirs, Joseph recalled fondly his father's last days and the personal loss he experienced: 'I sensed that the world was emptier for me and that a portion of my home had been transferred to the other world.' (*Milestones*, p 119.)

Two months later, in Castelgandolfo outside Rome, the nineteen-year pontificate of Pope Pius XII came to an end. At the conclave to elect his successor, held in the Sistine Chapel in October 1958, the choice of the cardinals fell on the Patriarch of Venice, Angelo Roncalli. The seventy-seven-year-old was to be a 'caretaker' Pope.

Pope Pius had pointedly avoided creating the Archbishop of Milan, Giovanni Montini a cardinal. Montini had served most of his life in the service of the Roman Curia before his unexpected transfer to Milan in 1954. In the minds of the cardinals, Montini was the one who seemed to possess the gifts necessary to succeed Pius. He was not, however, a cardinal. It was supposed that a new Pope would create Montini a cardinal, as his was a See which traditionally boasted a cardinal's hat. That is precisely what happened. In December, the newly elected John XXIII called a consistory. The first prelate he bestowed the red hat on was Giovanni Battisti Montini.

If the cardinals had expected a caretaker papacy, they soon found that they were mistaken. John had always been an avid student of history. When he ascended the papal throne, he realised that the church and the world needed a special message of consolation and hope. The uncertainty of the post-war years, the subsequent depression and rapidly expanding telecommunications posed both dilemmas and opportunities for the church.

On 25 January 1959, Pope John travelled to the Basilica of St Paul outside the Walls, where the 'apostle of the Gentiles' had been buried. He announced to the assembled cardinals his intention of convening a church council. The cardinals met his proposal with a stoney silence. After a few moments, the Pope observed: 'We would have expected greater enthusiasm from Your Eminences.'

John was nevertheless determined to proceed with his plan to hold an ecumenical council in Rome. The last council was the First Vatican Council held in 1871. Prior to that, the last council had been that of Trent, which took place in three sessions between 1545-63. John believed that councils should form a regular part of church life and not be called only when emergencies dictated, as had been the case in the past. Despite curial opposition, Pope John pressed on with his intention of convening the council and presiding over it.

Preparations took much longer than either John or his advisers had anticipated. The Curia had not been won over to the idea and sought to slow down progress by sending out mountains of preparatory documentation to the bishops of the world. Despite John's persistent encouragement to hasten their work, the various offices of the Vatican bureaucracy delayed the opening of the Second Vatican Council until October 1962. By that stage John was seriously ill with cancer, and although he opened the council, he was not to oversee its successful conclusion.

But the council itself engendered extraordinary excitement and interest throughout the Catholic Church and beyond. The bishops of the world were invited to submit proposals for discussion at the council. Thirteen committees were formed, composed of almost one thousand participants who met in a myriad of sub-committees. One of the cardinals who sat on the Central Preparatory Commission was Joseph Frings, Archbishop of Cologne. At regular intervals he received from the curial offices various *schemata*, or preparatory documents which were to be discussed on the council floor. Initially, the Curia expected that they would be able to 'rubber- stamp' the various initiatives which John had proposed and which had found support in some quarters. Cardinal Frings was one such ally. Enthused by John's vision, Frings gathered around him a small circle of advisers who read the drafts coming from Rome and made suggestions for subsequent revisions. One of the experts Frings involved was Joseph Ratzinger.

The period just prior to the opening of the council demonstrated the grounds for both optimism and pessimism which marked the beginning of the new decade. In 1960, a young man, John F. Kennedy had been elected president of the United States, the first Catholic to hold the position. In that same year the first International Conference for Disarmament, held at Geneva, broke down without any resolution. In 1962, the Berlin Wall was erected, raising the 'Iron Curtain' which would dominate European politics for almost three decades. South Africa broke away from the Commonwealth, accentuating its racist policies. The Soviets installed missiles on the island of Cuba, precipitating an international crisis.

It was against this background that the twenty-first Ecumenical Council opened. On a crisp day, 11 October 1962, Pope John XXIII was carried on the *sedia gestatoria*, the portable throne, into the Basilica, where over 2500 of the world's bishops had gathered. Most of the bishops had brought a secretary, and several had a *peritus*, or theological expert, to accompany them. While the Curia had sought to mould the deliberations on the council floor, the Pope had left only vague directions, which ensured the freedom of the bishops to dialogue and discuss the various *schemata* which were presented.

Cardinal Frings set off with his secretary Fr Luthe and Joseph Ratzinger. The university professor had to find cover for his lectures while he was at the council. Although he was not an official *peritus* or expert, Ratzinger was named to the position towards the end of the first session.

In an enlightened move, the governing council of cardinals decided to present a 'safe' topic to begin the council. The liturgy was so central to the Church's spiritual life that it was believed its *schema* would be discussed and passed quickly and without controversy. How wrong they were! From the beginning, several bishops expressed their dissatisfaction with the overweaning influence of the curial office which had drafted the *schema*. Nevertheless, the debates proceeded quite rapidly, with calls for a return to the simplicity of the 'Roman' liturgy being agreed by curial officials and the bishops alike.

Lodged in the German College at Santa Maria del Anima, beside Piazza Navona, the Germans soon threw themselves into the thick of things. In reality, many of the finest theologians of the time came from German-speaking countries. The young Dr Ratzinger enjoyed meeting up with intellectuals from all over the world.

Each morning the bishops met in St Peter's for Mass, followed by various speeches overseen by a committee of three cardinal presidents. The bishops sat in tiered seating which rose on either side of the main nave, from the back door to the altar. Above, in raised tribunes sat members of other churches and ecumenical guests. The senior bishops sat to the front. The tribute *seniores priores*, the older first, was to help those hard of hearing. A wag commented that deafness had never been regarded as an impediment for a bishop. Down towards the end of the basilica near the doors sat one of the youngest bishops, the Pole, Karol Wojtyla.

It soon became clear that the real work remained to be done. More and more of the bishops and their theological advisers were impatient with the slow pace at which some of the *schemata* were moving. Pope John chose not to attend the daily sessions in order to give the bishops greater freedom of speech, but he followed most of the sessions by close circuit in his apartments. On the very first day, the Curia had tried to impose its will by nominating the members of the conciliar commissions. One of those who vigorously opposed the suggestion was Cardinal Joseph Frings. Elections were postponed for three days, in order to ensure greater representation.

Only when the second document was presented for discussion did the theological temperature rise. Some of the Council Fathers believed that the Council of Trent had given the definitive word on the theological subject of Revelation. But others argued that progress in biblical studies and Patristics had greatly enhanced the understanding of the hitherto rigidly juridical and hierarchical structure of the church. Despite the generally favourable attitude to the discussions, it soon became clear that the view of the church as the 'people of God' would have serious repercussions for the structure and organisation of the church and its relationship in the world. Lines began to be drawn in the sand. The *schemata* drawn up by Cardinal Alfredo Ottavianni, Prefect of the Holy Office, were rejected out of hand as triumphalist and out of step with modern thinking. It was to this office, under its new name of the Congregation for the Doctrine of the Faith, that Joseph Ratzinger was to be appointed three decades later.

Cardinal Frings was deeply impressed by his theological adviser's acumen. He requested Ratzinger to draft a *schema* which he would present to other cardinals present in Rome. It was well received. The suggestion was made that the Jesuit Karl Rahner should be invited to rewrite the *schema* along with its author, Joseph Ratzinger. The two men had first met in 1956, at a conference on theology in Königstein. Each respected the other, but it soon became obvious that they came from polar opposite theological viewpoints. Ratzinger criticised Rahner for his overly philosophical slant. From his earliest days, Joseph Ratzinger had greatly valued theology over philosophy. Any theologian who place more emphasis on philosophers than theologians was suspect in his view. The final document was mostly Rahner's work, and Ratzinger was unhappy about the version which went before the bishops. Along with the official version, it was rejected, to Ratzinger's private relief.

Soon the reputations of the German-speaking theologians became well-known among the bishops attending the council. Few, if any, had brought advisers of such stature. Moreover, behind these theologians were centuries of scholarship, especially from the nineteenth and twentieth centuries. They had worked closely with Lutheran colleagues. This gave their work a particular edge. While some dazzled in public, Dr Ratzinger located the libraries he needed to support his work. In the mornings he became a regular visitor at the Germanicum, close by the Spanish Steps, a fine library of mainly German literature. Here he gathered the notes from books he needed to consult. In the afternoon he met with Cardinal Frings and any other guests the cardinal cared to invite. Quickly, Frings had gained a reputation for hosting a good stable of theologians and being very forward-looking.

When the first session of the council concluded on 8 December, there was little by way of concrete achievements. Those who had hoped that the Council would end there and then were disappointed to hear that a new session would commence some months later. On 3 June the following year, Pope John XXIII died of cancer. The reconvening of the council would depend on his successor.

Giovanni Battista Montini was elected Pope Paul VI (1963-78) on the sixth ballot of the two day conclave which followed John's death. Although he had spent the largest part of his life in the Vatican's Secretariat of State, he had nine years of pastoral experience as Archbishop of Milan. Thus his curial and diocesan experience gave him a considerable advantage over most other bishops. The curial cardinals had refrained from voting for Montini during the conclave, a fact of which Montini was well aware.

Pope Paul decided to reconvene the council as soon as was feasible. Once more the world's bishops and various theological advisers travelled to Rome. Over the remaining three sessions of the council, which closed on 5 December 1965, Ratzinger became a well-known public figure. Although he could not participate in any official debates, he wrote Cardinal Frings' interventions for him, gave interviews around Rome and took part in numerous symposia held in and around the city. He also published a set of commentaries on the proceedings which informed German readers about what was happening in Rome.

In the meantime, Joseph Ratzinger had made a further important change in his academic career. He had been noted as an important adviser to Cardinal Frings by the German-speaking bishops. But with his newly-acquired fame came another difficult decision. The previous year, Hermann Volk had been made bishop of Mainz. He was a noted scholar and had held the chair of dogma at the University of Münster. This was now vacant, and Ratzinger was tempted to apply for the position. There was no doubt that the position held greater prestige for Dr Ratzinger. On a personal level, his departure would make life easier for a number of his students. In Bonn, Joseph Ratzinger had encountered jealousy among other faculty members. Although they did not attack him openly, he learned that his doctoral candidates were being victimised by his colleagues. Rankled by their petty-mindedness and prompted by memories of his own habilitation anxieties some years earlier, he decided that Münster offered the best of both worlds.

In the summer of 1963, Joseph moved to Münster. He had promised Cardinal Frings that he would continue to attend sessions of the Second Vatican Council in the autumn. He expected that the council would finish before Christmas, so that he could continue his academic career in Münster.

It was to prove an exhausting promise. Despite improvement in transport, the to-ing and fro-ing between Münster and Rome took its toll. By now, media interest had grown considerably in the proceedings of the council. Somewhat superficial divisions were made in media circles, which Ratzinger did not believe corresponded to the truth. In particular, the young theologian was uncomfortable with the divisions between progressive and conservative bishops and theologians.

When Pope Paul opened the second session of the council on 29 September 1963, he had set an agenda more precise than anything Roncalli had suggested. Pope Paul had been alarmed by the conservatives who warned that the council could easily end in schism. He requested the bishops to examine the dogmatic nature of the church, its renewal, its ecumenical focus and relations with the world.

But the very crisis proved stimulation for theologians who continued to flock to Rome to offer their suggestions. Küng, Conger, De Lubac and Chenu all became familiar faces in the salons of the Eternal City, offering stimulating advice as the council sailed into ever-stormier waters.

The *schema* on the pastoral office of bishops was rejected by the bishops who sent it back to the central committee to be rewritten. The debate on 'separated brethren' soon broadened into a discussion of anti-Semitism, which had come to a head during the Second World War. Bishops from Catholic countries listened to missionary bishops recount their experiences, while it became apparent that an abyss of misunderstanding existed between them on various issues.

The session concluded with the promulgation of *Sacrosanctam Concilium*, the decree on the liturgy, and *Inter Mirifica*, the decree on Social Communications. The former was soon to have an extraordinary impact on Catholic worship, and within a decade the Catholic liturgy was transformed almost beyond recognition.

But there was hope in gestures. In January 1964, Pope Paul made a ground-breaking visit to the Holy Land. It was the first international visit in centuries. In December of that year, Pope Paul met the Ecumenical Patriarch Athenagoras, and the two men opened a new era of ecumenical dialogue.

On a personal note, the Ratzinger family had cause to celebrate. In February 1964, Georg Ratzinger succeeded Theobald Schrems as director of the Regensburg Cathedral Choir. It was a prestigious appointment, which was to occupy him at the centre of Regensburg's liturgical life until his retirement. There was some sadness, for now the happy period at Traunstein came to an end. Henceforward, the choirmaster's home in Regensburg became the focal point of meetings of the three siblings.

The third session of the Council opened on 14 September 1964 and lasted until 21 November. The Council Fathers were anxious to move rapidly through the remaining *schemata*, on the priesthood, laity, lay apostolate, missions and education. The proposed decree on the laity was sent back to the central committee at once for rewriting as there was no recognition that their vocation came from baptism. The most important *schema* that remained was *Lumen Gentium, The Church in the Modern World*. Even its title was controversial. An earlier working title was 'The Church *and* the Modern World'. There was controversy also about the question of collegiality, or how the bishops of the world were to work as a body united to the See of Peter. Ratzinger took a position in favour of collegiality – the governance of the church by the Pope in communion with all the bishops. He made a significant contribution to articles 22 and 23 which dealt with collegiality. He also worked on the editorial committee which rewrote the decree on the missionary activity of the church. He underlined that all Christians have, by virtue of their baptism, the duty and privilege of promoting and spreading the faith, long seen by the laity as the preserve of priests and religious.

There was pressure to bring the council to an end. Many bishops were afraid that it might turn into a mini-Trent. While hoteliers and restauranteurs rejoiced at the presence of the bishops and their entourages, the Vatican was already feeling the financial pinch of hosting the council. The fourth and final session took place in St Peter's between 14 September and 8 December 1965.

The Pope announced that a synod of bishops would be established which could be convened at regular intervals. This seemed an honourable way out of the impasse as to when the council could end. It would always remain under the thumb, however, of the Roman pontiff. Debates on the position of bishops, of the renewal of religious life and religious liberty all continued apace although Pope Paul intervened on the question of priestly celibacy, closing further debate. He later withdrew the question of human fertility from the council floor. The council finally ended on 8 December, three days after the Pope and Ecumenical Patriarch Athenagoras had 'consigned to oblivion' the mutual excommunication of each church in 1054.

Now the real challenge lay ahead for the papacy. The implementation of the decrees was left to the Bishop of Rome. A plethora of documents emanated from the Vatican in the months and years following the Vatican Council. The Pope also spoke through gestures. On 23 March 1966, he welcomed the Archbishop of Canterbury, Michael Ramsey, at the Vatican. Both men exchanged rings. To this day, every time an archbishop of Canterbury meets the Pope he wears Pope Paul VI's ring. On 25 July 1967 he met with Athenagoras I at Istanbul and later that year, on 26 October, he received him at the Vatican.

CHAPTER SIX

Back to Academia

By summer Joseph Ratzinger had returned to Germany to a new teaching position in Tübingen. Already he had been approached in 1959 to apply for the chair of fundamental theology, which he had turned down. Now a second offer came his way. A new chair in dogma had been created. Among those who had proposed him for the new position was the well-known Swiss theologian, Hans Küng. The two had meet in 1957 at a congress of dogmatic theologians in Austria. They had met again at the Second Vatican Council. Despite initial warmth, their relationship was destined to cool during those Roman years as they debated issues raised at the Council.

The period of teaching at Tübingen was at first highly satisfactory for Ratzinger. Although he was rather unhappy about his cramped apartments, he was nearer his brother Georg in Regensburg. After the exhausting years of the council, Ratzinger's health was now very fragile. He found that he had little energy. When he was free for a weekend, he took the train to visit Georg and listen to the famous choir. On other occasions, when there was a break in teaching commitments, he picnicked with friends and colleagues in the Black Forest. Slowly he regained his health.

During this period, he was assigned to teach a course on Christology by the Dean. His classes drew large crowds of students. They were impressed by his openness and his knowledge of Lutheran authors, some of whom were his colleagues. In 1967, at the end of his second semester, Tübingen celebrated the 150th anniversary of its foundation. The following year, however, the university, as with many others throughout the world, was to experience the revolt subsequently referred to as 'the year of 68'. Ratzinger later laid the blame on the absorption of existentialism into theology and the mingling of Marxist philosophy. But the so-called revolution was by no means confined to theology. Every department of every university experienced the change in some form or another. For Ratzinger, however, the revolt was based in students' demands for unrealistic change wrought by their own desires, rather than in obedience to God's will.

Ratzinger had now been teaching for a decade, in three prestigious universities. What was happening on the world stage was not just a student revolt. He suspected that there was also a political motivation behind it. What offended him was the manner in which his own students began to ridicule elements of the church's teaching, which he saw as synonymous with the faith.

During this period he published his first major work, *An Introduction to Christianity*. It was a summation of his ten years of teaching experience and was developed from the 1966-67 series of lectures in Tübingen.

The constant struggle at the university of Tübingen was beginning to tell on Ratzinger's health. He was dean of his faculty, a member of the governing senate and one of the committee charged with drawing up a new constitution. His lectures had been interrupted and he had been challenged in public by students. The sudden collapse of respect for his status as a lecturer was an affront, but the lack of respect to the priesthood was more shocking. Although he later admitted that the revolt was planned and executed by a relatively small group, he found it difficult to cope with the changes. Moreover, he was disappointed by the lack of support he received from the senior members of the faculty.

Shortly after Christmas of that year, Joseph received an invitation from the newly-established University of Regensburg. He had come to know the small city from his regular visits to his brother. He had already been offered the first chair of dogma, which had been taken by his former colleague Johann Auer. Now, when the offer came for a second chair, he seized the opportunity. The constant friction was too much for him at Tübingen. Now it was no longer the students in revolt. The very faculty was at war with itself. The atmosphere of tension and bitterness was too much for Joseph. He had never dreamed academia could be so small-minded and petty. With few regrets, he decided to leave Tübingen for Regensburg.

This move, Joseph Ratzinger hoped, would be his last. Since childhood he had moved several times. Now, aged 47, it was time to settle down in one university and prepare for the mature years. The success of his *Introduction to Christianity* gave him an appetite to publish more. He had discovered a skill and gift for writing which he had never previously considered. Although the building of the campus was still under way, Joseph soon began to feel at home. His brother arranged dinners for him, inviting friends to his home. There was an air of joviality. The university soon gained a good reputation. It did not seem so buffeted as other universities by the various ideologies which Ratzinger felt were opposed to education and indeed the Christian faith. International students enrolled on the course, offering stimulation both to fellow students and the professors themselves. This was perhaps Ratzinger the theologian's most satisfactory period. Already in 1964, he had helped found a new journal for theologians, called *Concilium*. The first number had been issued the following year. Regarded as a serious publication, it had further cemented Ratzinger's reputation in Germany and abroad.

In July of that same year, Pope Paul VI published an encyclical, *Humanae Vitae*. It was a meditation on the dignity of marriage and the human family. Although several passages were later seen to be prophetic, the encyclical as a whole received a cool and sometimes hostile reception. Within weeks of its publication, several bishops' conferences published pastoral commentaries on the contents of the Pope's work. Never before had the bishops felt the need to gloss a papal encyclical in such a public and universal manner. The focus of the commentaries had to do with artificial birth control, which the Pope had ruled against. A committee to examine the controversial area had been set up by Pope John XXIII. Leaks from the committee suggested that Pope Paul might take a broader line than in the past. In the event, the Pope was quite clear in his disapproval. Various national bishops' conferences wrote on the superiority of conscience. Montini was bruised by the public distancing of several bishops. He never wrote another papal encyclical.

Further recognition was to come shortly after his arrival in Regensburg when the Bavarian theologian was appointed a member of the International Theological Commission. This body had been set up by Pope Paul VI in order to facilitate the implementation of the decrees of the Second Vatican Council in the theological sphere. Many of the changes proposed by the Council Fathers had been passed in theoretical form in the sixteen decrees. In order for them to be brought into reality, a theological framework would be needed. It was the suggestion of the bishops themselves that such a body, composed of international theologians and other experts, be established. Cologne's Cardinal Frings suggested Ratzinger's name to Pope Paul. The Pope, despite the fact that he had spent much of his life in Vatican diplomacy, appreciated the need to expand the international aspect of the Vatican. The imbalance had been caused by the fact that for over four centuries the papacy had been occupied by Italian Popes. The unprecedented coverage by the media necessitated a wider cast of talent.

For Ratzinger, the yearly meetings in Rome introduced him once more to the broader stage of scholarship as well as making important contacts in the Vatican. The Committee made a significant impact on the development of the documents which Pope Paul issued in the subsequent years implementing the decrees of the Second Vatican Council.

There was one thing which troubled Joseph Ratzinger deeply. In 1970 the *Novus Ordo Missae* was introduced by Pope Paul VI. Effectively the work of Archbishop Annabile Bugnini, it was a simplification of the Mass. Liturgical scholars hailed it as an important development in the celebration of the Eucharist. No longer was there simply one form of Mass, but a rich choice drawn from centuries of experience. Instead of simply celebrating the Roman canon, there were now three others. One was based on a Eucharistic text written in the second century by Hippolytus, and two others were newly composed. The various prayers of the Mass were rearranged, as indeed was the form of the liturgical calendar. But the most significant innovation was the language used in the celebration of the Mass. For most of its history, the Mass was celebrated in Latin, the common language of the people where it developed. The bishops argued that a vernacular form was needed. Although Latin was a ringing symbol of the universality of the church, it had become incomprehensible to most modern worshippers. While it made sense to preserve this form of worship in the heartland of Europe – at least as an option – it was unreasonable to oblige Chinese priests or African priests or any other non-Latin speaking population to learn the parts of the Mass in a dead language.

At the Second Vatican Council, Joseph Ratzinger had been critical of the church's exclusive use of Latin, both in its liturgy and its formation of clergy. He welcomed the celebration of an Eastern-rite liturgy in Greek in St Peter's during the first session of the council. He was critical of the perceived sterility of Latin, even though he himself was an elegant and fluent speaker of the language. He encouraged the broader use of languages and other rites.

Writing in 1998 in his memoirs, the then Cardinal Ratzinger repented somewhat of his former zeal for novelty in the liturgy: 'I was not able to see that the negative side of the liturgical movement would afterwards re-emerge with redoubled strength, almost to the point of pushing the liturgy to its own self-destruction.' However, on his visit to the tomb of St Paul-outside-the-Walls on 25 April 2005, the newly-elected pontiff chose to lead the liturgy in Italian, even though the booklet had been prepared with the text in Latin. As bishop of Rome, he wished to speak to the people in their own language, not in that of their ancestors.

Although Joseph Ratzinger lived frugally, he was persuaded by friends to buy a house for his retirement. He had a good salary and also had made money from his conferences and writings. For several years he had lived a rather nomadic existence, changing house frequently as he took up new posts. Accordingly he acquired a residence in Pentling, to the west of Regensburg. His sister Maria came to live with him. Here he was within easy distance of the university and finally had somewhere of his own to put his ever-increasing library.

His literary output continued. By the early 1970s, Ratzinger had become somewhat disillusioned with the editorship of *Concilium*. He had begun to part ways with Hans Küng, Karl Rahner and Edward Schillebeeckx.

Along with other eminent theologians, Henri de Lubac, Walter Kasper, Karl Lehmann and Hans Urs von Balthasar, he founded another journal, *Communio*. It is interesting that of the original founders, Kasper, Lehmann and Ratzinger became cardinals. Urs von Balthasar died two days before he was to be created a cardinal by Pope John Paul II. A decade later, as Prefect of the Congregation of the Doctrine of the Faith, Ratzinger was to formally censure parts of the theology of Küng and Schillebeeckx on behalf of Pope John Paul.

CHAPTER SEVEN

Bishop and Cardinal

Life continued tranquilly for Dr Ratzinger throughout the decade. In the spring of March 1977, the papal nuncio called to see him in Regensburg. Ratzinger already suspected the reason for the visit. The archbishop of Munich, Cardinal Julius Döpfner had died the previous July. Within days of the former archbishop's funeral, the name of Joseph Ratzinger was being circulated by the diocesan gossips. He had the profile judged by many of the period to make a good archbishop. The Vatican preferred to choose as bishops priests who had a good theological background. Further studies were virtually a prerequisite. Joseph Ratzinger had made a mark in Germany in scholarly circles, but more importantly, he had made a good impression in Rome.

The nuncio handed the professor a letter and explained that it came from the Pope. He took his leave but asked Ratzinger to confirm if he would accept the position within a day or two. For the theologian, this was a private disaster. All his years of study and scholarly research seemed to evaporate in front of the vision of a mitre and crozier. He thought of the various reasons why he would not be suitable for the pastoral situation. That night he talked to his brother Georg and to his confessor, Fr Auer. Hopes that he would be advised by his counsellors not to take the episcopal ministry were dashed when Auer told him plainly 'You must accept.' He called to the nuncio the next day in his hotel. There, on hotel stationery, he wrote his letter of acceptance.

The date for the episcopal consecration was set for 28 May. It was a magnificent day in the austere cathedral of Munich. The new archbishop was the first diocesan priest to be consecrated bishop in 80 years. Pope Paul, who personally appointed him, recalled Ratzinger as a reliable and brilliant theologian. Paul was elderly, and was to die the following year. His choice of the Bavarian theologian determined Ratzinger's future career and ultimately the road which led to the papal throne. Munich was traditionally a cardinalatial See. A month later, the Archbishop of Munich was in Rome to receive the red hat.

Although Ratzinger had several years of academic administration, the day to day running of a diocese was something quite different. In the German system, however, a vicar general was responsible for overseeing the vast administration of the diocese. Part of taxes paid by citizens are delivered to churches or charities. The vast majority pay their taxes to the denomination to which they belong. Ratzinger soon gained a reputation as a pastoral bishop, travelling throughout the diocese to celebrate the sacraments.

On 6 August, Pope Paul VI died in his country residence of Castelgandolfo, some 18 miles south of Rome. The cardinals were called to Rome to celebrate his funeral and elect a new successor to Peter. On 25 August, one hundred and eleven cardinals entered the cramped quarters surrounding the Sistine Chapel. Under rules laid down by the late Pope, only cardinals who had not reached their 80th birthday could enter the conclave to elect a Pope. In the great edifice built by Pope Sixtus IV (1471-84) they would cast their votes four times a day until a candidate gained two thirds plus one of the votes. With this majority he would be elected 263rd bishop of Rome.

The choice of a new Pope was seen as a daunting task. For two weeks following the death of Pope Paul, the cardinals had held daily meetings. For many, it was the first time they had met. The implementation of the Second Vatican Council had not gone as smoothly as the participants had hoped. Some had detected, in the final years of Pope Paul, cracks in the very fabric of the church. Paul himself, in a memorable phase, had referred to the 'smoke of Satan' which had infiltrated the church. What was needed was somebody who would carry forward the momentum generated by the council. But the church also needed a clear presentation of doctrine. The last decade of Montini's pontificate had been marred by the hostile reaction in some quarters to his encyclical on marriage, *Humanae Vitae*. Pope Paul had presided over a successful Jubilee Year in 1975. His last years were dominated by crippling pain caused by severe arthritis and divergences between progressives and conservatives which caused him mental anguish. Although there had been speculation that the cardinals might break four centuries of tradition to elect a non-Italian, in the event they once more chose an Italian. Albino Luciani, the Patriarch of Venice, was elected on the second day of voting, at the fourth ballot. The new pontiff took the name John Paul, in memory of John XXIII who had made him a bishop and Paul VI who had created him a cardinal. The new Pope had a pleasing, if timid personality. Although he showed little understanding of the Roman Curia, he had the popular touch which immediately won the hearts of all who heard him.

One of his first acts was to request the Bavarian cardinal to travel to Equador to represent him at the Shrine of Our Lady of Guayquil at centenary celebrations. It was Ratzinger's first trip to Latin America but already he felt he knew a sufficient amount about the political situation to make an address critical of the way in which the church was developing in the area. He had come to suspect a movement which had been developing throughout the decade, liberation theology. In the subsequent years, he would become a vociferous opponent of the movement in the church which, faced with encroaching poverty, had scant regard for the status quo. While some theorists might argue even for violent action to overthrow corrupt régimes, Cardinal Ratzinger repeatedly rejected calls for such extremism. It was to place him in direct confrontation with both his colleagues and pastoral workers throughout Latin America.

But Luciani's pontificate was not destined to last. Just a month after his election, Pope John Paul I died suddenly. His body was discovered on the early morning of 28 September by a religious sister. It appeared that he had died of a coronary thrombosis.

Once more the cardinals were summoned to Rome to preside over a papal funeral and once more enter conclave. Smarting under the rapidity of Luciani's demise, the cardinals thought through more carefully their next choice. Already it emerged in the days following his funeral that Pope John Paul I had suffered with health problems even before his election. After the lengthy pontificate of Paul VI, who had died at the age of 81 and the short pontificate of John Paul, it seemed wise to select a healthy, and preferably younger candidate.

Meeting daily in the interim while waiting for the conclave to begin, the cardinals began to take stock of their colleagues, scrutinising each other more carefully than they had a month earlier. For a second time in a month, the world media had focused global attention on the papal elections. One of the points which the media continued to make of the 'smiling Pope' was his ease with people. Now the chain of generations of diplomats had been broken, perhaps there would be a chance to elect another pastorally sensitive pontiff?

One of the 'king-makers' at the conclave was Vienna's archbishop, Franz König. He began to sound out the other cardinals about their feelings. To several he suggested the name of Karol Wojtyla, the archbishop of Krakow. He was young at fifty-eight. He had taken part in the Second Vatican Council. He had proved himself a tough negotiator with the Communist authorities in his native Poland. A man with acting talents, he moreover was gifted with languages. When König approached Cardinal Stefan Wyszñski, the Primate of Poland recoiled. 'Me? But the Communists would see it as a victory if I went to Rome to become Pope!' When the Austrian cardinal explained that he had been thinking of Wojtyla, Wyszñski dismissed the suggestion out of hand. 'He is too young and nobody knows him outside of Poland.'

Once more a decision was reached on the fourth ballot, on the second day of the conclave. Karol Wojtyla emerged as the new Pope. Taking the name John Paul in honour of his predecessor, he presented himself as a 'man from afar'. Over the next twenty-six and a half years, he was to govern the church as no other pontiff had done in history, raising the stature of the papacy immeasurably.

The first sign of Pope John Paul's interest in and esteem for Cardinal Ratzinger came in 1980. The Synod of Bishops was due to take place that year. The Pope normally appointed a 'relator' to the Synod. It was a technical term, rather akin to chairman of the preparatory and executive committee. The choice of a non-curial cardinal both continued Paul's vision for a more international administration of the Curia and John Paul's esteem for the German prelate. Wojtyla was first and foremost a philosopher by training. He realised his need for a dependable and talented theologian at his side. Karol Wojtyla had first been elected to the Council for the Synod of Bishops in 1971 and had gained a good understanding of how the sessions worked.

A special Synod for the Dutch Church had been convened in Rome in January of that same year. The summonsing of such an unusual event sent alarm signals to several branches in the church.This Polish pontiff meant business. Rumours had reached Rome in the preceding years that the seven Dutch bishops were not doing their jobs properly. Division was rife in Holland. When the Synod opened in Rome, the bishops found that not only had the three presidents of the Synod been chosen by the Pope, but that six other cardinals, close collaborators with the Pope, had been appointed.

Just some months earlier, in October 1978, Cardinal Ratzinger had vetoed the appointment of his erstwhile colleague, Johannes Metz to the chair of theology at the University of Munich. Under the terms of the 1924 Concordat between the Holy See and Bavaria, the local bishop had the right of veto on teaching appointments. The reason the cardinal made the veto remained secret, but it became obvious that Ratzinger was disturbed by elements of Metz's 'liberation theology'. Reaction in academic circles was furious. Kark Rahner wrote to Ratzinger accusing him of 'senseless, unscientific manipulation'. But the public metal of Ratzinger the bishop had been tested. In Rome, his tenacity was noted as a further bombshell hit the German academic community. On 15 December, the Swiss theologian Hans Küng had his licence to teach as a Catholic theologian withdrawn by the Congregation for the Doctrine of the Faith. The German bishops immediately published, within two days, a statement defending Rome's stance.

The 1980 Synod was the Pope's first ordinary Synod. He chose the theme of the family. The *lineamenta*, or document sent out to the world's bishops before the synod began, was tedious and longwinded. More than one bishop complained that the trip to Rome could have been saved just by publishing the *lineamenta*. Within three weeks of the Synod's opening on 26 September, the bishops had run into trouble. Frustrated by rambling interjections, a group of bishops asked to meet Cardinal Ratzinger privately. They suggested that the only way of moving forward was to send a list of proposals to the Pope. Cardinal Ratzinger consulted the Pope who agreed. But their proposals seemed to go nowhere. The Pope ignored most of them in his final address on 25 October when he bade the participants farewell.

It was now up to Cardinal Ratzinger to collate the materials and suggestions made over the month. It had become practice for the Pope to write an apostolic constitution following a Synod. What happened when the Pope did not agree with all that the bishops had said? The answer lay in *Familiaris Consortio*, the post Synodal document published on 15 December 1981. In it, Pope John Paul reiterated his teaching on family life and sexuality, while selecting some themes which had been covered by the bishops at the Synod.

Meanwhile, the Pope had chosen quite bravely to travel to Germany in November 1980. For a Polish pontiff to make a visit on German soil presented sensitive diplomatic issues. Just five days before the Pope's arrival in Bonn, one hundred and thirteen German-speaking theologians delivered a letter to the papal nuncio. The letter was a bold request to the Pope on several issues. It called for a new interpretation of the church's teaching on birth control, softening on inter-church discipline for married couples, a review of the pastoral treatment of the divorced, the ordination of women and a review of the role of the Congregation for the Doctrine of the Faith. The Pope publicly ignored the contents of the letter and no reply was sent.

The papal visit concluded in Bavaria. He visited the Marian shrine of Altötting, near Joseph Ratzinger's birthplace. Then he continued to Munich, Ratzinger's diocese. Here the Pope celebrated Mass for the youth of the area. A young girl, Barbara Engl gave an address of welcome. Departing from her prepared text, she made a plea for the ordination of women and the end of obligatory celibacy. The addition had already been vetoed by Cardinal Ratzinger's office, but the young girl made the addition regardless. The Pope did not comment on her address. Cardinal Ratzinger was furious. It was, he said later, one of the most embarrassing moments of his life. Pope John Paul had made it quite clear during his German visit that there would be no change and he remained determined in this throughout the rest of his pontificate.

But by now, Joseph Ratzinger had made a deep impression on Pope John Paul. The pontiff wanted to call him to Rome to serve in the Curia. The obvious place for him was the Congregation for Catholic Education. Ratzinger had all the right qualifications. As soon as the post would become vacant, the Pope decided, he would send for Ratzinger. In place of the usual career diplomat, Pope John Paul would be able to place a qualified professor who had fine track record. But Pope John Paul changed his mind. When Cardinal Franjo Seper resigned in 1981, the Pope made a surprise move. Joseph Ratzinger would replace him as the new Prefect for the Congregation for the Doctrine of the Faith. Here too curial careerists had reigned supreme. Pope John Paul made a daring and innovative appointment. It was clear that he intended placing highly qualified men in key positions.

On 25 November 1981, Joseph Ratzinger was named Prefect. He received the news in a letter forwarded to him by the papal nuncio. It was another upheaval and one which he did not relish. But in obedience he accepted it and moved to Rome definitively in early 1982.

CHAPTER EIGHT

Congregation for the Doctrine of the Faith

The office into which the new Prefect moved was formerly known as the Holy Office. It lies to the left of St Peter's Basilica and is housed in a large sixteenth-century building. The history of the Congregation dates back to 1542, when Pope Paul III (1534-49) established a set of six cardinals to deal with doctrinal matters. It was the aftermath of the Reformation and the Catholic Church was still reeling from the dramatic split which had caused enormous losses in numbers and prestige. Heresy was rampant in Rome's eyes. The Congregation was amplified once more under Pope Paul IV (1555-59) in 1555, one of the first fruits of the Council of Trent. It took its present form in 1965 when Pope Paul VI renamed it the Congregation for the Doctrine of the Faith. It's most recent reform came in 2001 when Pope John Paul modified it once more.

Presided over by the Cardinal Prefect, the Congregation governs anything to do with the content of the Catholic faith. By its very nature, it deals rather more with controversy than with anything else. It is most controversially known for its disciplining of theologians whose teaching is judged to be incompatible with the Catholic faith. Such publicised events form a miniscule part of the Congregation's function. It examines cases such as apparitions, supernatural happenings, admission to or expulsion from the ministry, the imposition and removal of the ban of excommunication, the setting up or closing of religious orders, offences against the Catholic faith and abuses of the celebration of the sacraments. All documents prepared by other Vatican offices, including the writings of the Pope himself, routinely pass through the office to be examined to ensure that their writings contain no hint of heresy or anything likely to cause confusion. A separate office deals with issues relating to the sacrament of matrimony. Two other institutions are presided over by the Prefect. These are the International Theological Committee and the International Biblical Commission. The former deals with theological developments while the latter examines insights and advances in biblical scholarship.

In the vaults of the building are kept the archives, containing documents which date back to the sixteenth century. The remainder of the documents are kept in the Vatican Secret Archives near the Vatican Galleries. The building also houses books and journals which are of use in the Congregation's work.

It was to this office that Joseph Ratzinger came in early 1982. He was assisted, as in all Congregations, by a Secretary, who administers the office on a daily basis. The staff varies between thirty-five and forty, although there is also a large number of external advisers and consulters who read and prepare documents for publication.

One of the first controversial documents Cardinal Joseph Ratzinger was obliged to sign was the notification confirming the excommunication of Archbishop Pierre Martin Ngo Dinh Thuc, formerly bishop of Hue in Vietnam. He had participated in the ordination of priests and bishops without the approval of the Holy See. For over a century, the Vatican had reserved to itself the right to appoint bishops to dioceses throughout the world. Although it was in stark contrast to the practice of the early church, where local clergy and people elected their own bishops, this was the result of centuries of papal centralisation. The move against the bishop was dramatic.

Dinh Thuc, a brother of the first president of Vietnam, was a traditionalist who had refused to accept the developments in the Catholic Church following the Second Vatican Council. He had come to know the French rebel Archbishop Marcel Lefebvre, who had founded a traditionalist seminary at Ecône in Switzerland. Here students were prepared for the priesthood according to the norms which applied before the Second Vatican Council.

Archbishop Thuc travelled to Spain to ordain some breakaway clerics, including an anti-Pope, Gregory XVIII. When the Vatican was informed of the consecration in violation of canon law, the Congregation for the Doctrine of the Faith was obliged to confirm his automatic sentence of excommunication. He repented publicly his action and the sentence of excommunication was lifted. But shortly afterwards he resumed his activities, which incurred renewed automatic excommunication. The disgraced archbishop moved to Rochester in New York, where he died in 1984. Shortly before his death he was reconciled with the church and received a special blessing from Pope John Paul.

During this time, the Congregation for the Doctrine of the Faith maintained a constant dialogue with the traditionalists headed by Archbishop Marcel Lefebvre. Ratzinger found himself privately in sympathy with many of the archbishop's complaints. His particular love of the liturgy made him an enthusiastic supporter of whatever could beautify it. Although he had argued during the Second Vatican Council that the liturgy needed to be stripped of many of its baroque excesses, he was dismayed at the abuses which flourished in the aftermath of the council. This, Ratzinger believed, was partly because of a defective formation of the clergy. A deplorable result of the 1968 revolutions was not only a decrease in respect for institutions. It was also a general decline in intellectual standards in seminaries among faculty and seminarians. In later years, Ratzinger argued that it was unwise suddenly to ban the use of the Rite which had formed over centuries and had nourished the people.

On 29 September 1983, the Sixth Synod of Bishops opened at the Vatican. This was the second to be held under Pope John Paul. The theme selected by the Pope was 'Reconciliation and Penance in the Church's Mission'. Shocked by the decline in penitents availing of the Sacrament of Reconciliation and Penance, Pope John Paul had decided to concentrate the Synods as far as possible on the celebration of the sacraments. Following the liturgical reforms carried out by Pope Paul VI, there were three forms of administering the sacrament available to priests. It went without saying that only priests could administer the sacrament, even though contemporary theologians had asserted that the practice of the early church had not restricted it to priests alone.

The three forms were quite clearly stated on paper, but in pastoral practice they were greatly confused. The most common form envisaged by the church was private absolution. This required a penitent to confess individually their sins to a priest who granted absolution and set a symbolic penance. Communal liturgies could be arranged to focus the attention of the parish on sin, but the individual confession to a priest was still part of the ceremony. Thirdly, in restricted circumstances, a general absolution could be granted. This had been enshrined in liturgical practice only in the most unusual cases, in the case of war or some other danger. In effect, it had gained considerable favour with the world's Catholics.

Cardinal Ratzinger had been named by the Pope as one of the Presidents of the Synod. To have made him relator once more would have been unwise. The cardinal listened to the numerous bishops who testified to their positive experience of the third rite. Many bishops in mission territories urged greater freedom for the third rite where there was an acute shortage of clergy. The Pope also listened with increasing irritation. It was inconceivable that the traditional form could be so rapidly abandoned. The Pope instructed Ratzinger to deliver an address in which he underlined the tradition of the church and set aright the correct application of the liturgical norms. In case anybody was left in any doubt about John Paul's views, the Pope canonised a Croatian Capuchin friar, Leopold Mandic, who had spent most of each day in a confessional in Padua. The date chosen was 16 October, the fifth anniversary of his own election as Pope.

With the closing of the second Synod under Pope John Paul, the bishops clearly understood where the Pope stood. He was determinedly on the side of orthodoxy and would be rigorous in his application of it. Offenders would be either punished or sidelined. It fell to Cardinal Ratzinger to ensure that the world's bishops carried out the papal mandate.

While the Synod was still in its early stages, Cardinal Ratzinger sent a letter, dated 4 October, to Archbishop Raymond G. Hunthausen of Seattle. The Vatican had received numerous complaints, mostly from anonymous sources, that the archbishop had permitted several liturgical and pastoral abuses to grow in his diocese. The Prefect notified Archbishop Hunthausen that an apostolic visitation would take place to review his stewardship.

This was a highly unusual step. Apostolic visitations were only invoked in the most serious of cases. The direction for the visitation had come directly from the Pope. It was to put John Paul on his first collision course with the church in the United States. Hunthausen could have expected such a move. As a conscientious objector, he strenuously opposed the armaments deals being promoted by the Reagan government. He withheld fifty per cent of his taxes in a nominal protest against the heavy US military build-up. This was only part of the story. Now the Vatican was surveying the role of women in the administration of parishes. The role of nuns in particular was being examined by the Congregation for Religious. The benign welcome extended to the Polish pontiff by Americans was rapidly evaporating.

In Europe, Cardinal Ratzinger turned his attention to the Masons. On 26 November 1983, the Congregation for the Doctrine of the Faith published the 'Declaration on Masonic Associations'. It was a short document, succinct and to the point. In 1981, a secret list had been found when the Italian police had raided the home of Lucio Gelli, a prominent member of the P2 Masonic Lodge. The newspapers were full of conspiracy stories, claiming that the list of members which had been found included cardinals who took part in the clandestine rituals. The Congregation's decision was clear. No Catholic could be a Mason, as it was incompatible with the faith. Those who remained members after the publication were barred from receiving Communion. The document stirred up considerable controversy but it died down after some weeks. Those who were members of the Masonic Lodges had to deal with the matter in a conscientious way, which meant leaving the organisation. But now Ratzinger's greatest challenge lay ahead.

CHAPTER NINE

Liberation Theology

At the Second Vatican Council, an appeal was made by the bishops for the church to take a clear stand in favour of the poor. Throughout the two thousand year history of Christianity, care for the underprivileged and weak members of society was a hallmark of its profession of faith. However, it was also true that certain sections of the church had failed to protect the vulnerable from exploitation. A case in point was to be found in Latin America. Since the opening of the continent to Europe in the sixteenth century, much of its subsequent history was of exploitation of the poor by the increasingly rich. Millions were sold into slavery as a result of the colonisation by the Portuguese and Spanish. With the exception of Bartolomeo de las Casas and some other missionaries, the church could be accused of often ignoring the plight of so many men, women and children for whom life was a toil and endless drudgery.

In 1968, the bishops of Latin America met at Medellín, Colombia. In their final message, they acknowledged that in the history of their own continent, Christians had often courted the rich rather than ameliorate the plight of the poor. For that reason they urged the church, at least in their own territories, to have a 'preferential option for the poor'. Soon it became a catchphrase as various communities took up the cry. Throughout the region, base communities were established to give a sense of solidarity and intimacy to worshippers, many of whom felt alienated by the forms of European liturgy in their parishes. This took on momentum as the Mass was increasingly celebrated in their native tongue and they heard the Bible in a language they could easily understand. Soon thinkers began to develop a 'liberation theology' closely modelled on the history of God's people as narrated in the Bible.

While many in the Latin American church enthusiastically embraced the new emphasis, others were dismayed by what they considered an unacceptable element of Marxist ideology. It was not enough simply to speak about structures of abuse. These had to be tackled. If necessary, violence might have to be employed. Elements within the broader strata of society would have to be persuaded to change the status quo.

As theologians meditated on this message, some saw that a logical step might involve dismantling the unjust structures of society. Some church-run schools catered for the wealthy rather than care for the poor. This was therefore a form of violence. Just as the whole community suffered, so, argued some theologians, the whole community had to find an answer. Today's Christian was urged to shape a fairer world. The world seems to be eternally unbalanced, but it is the Christian challenge to set that right.

To Pope John Paul, such developments seemed dangerous. Although at a General Audience held after his return from Central America in 1983, the Pope claimed that liberation theology was at the heart of the church, he evidently mistrusted some elements of it. He had lived through the oppressive and unjust Nazi and Communist régimes. To fight violence with violence, as was advocated by Marxist ideologists, was unacceptable. Karl Marx had called for the violent overthrow of the ruling classes. History itself had proven that such a universal upheaval was even beyond the power of the most zealous Marxist.

Joseph Ratzinger also had strong reservations. He too had lived through the Nazi régime. He had experienced the traumatic Marxist summer of 1968. He had also seen his own country split in two.

A number of priests and religious in Latin America embraced the armed struggle. For both Pope and Prefect, this was appalling. Equally they were shocked by reports to the Vatican of priests who refused the sacraments to members of their congregation who failed to embrace their 'preferential option for the poor'.

Ratzinger dubbed that option an 'empty catchphrase'. He did not believe that it expressed the full meaning of the Christian message. He discussed his worries with the Pope in the late winter of 1984. A clear restatement of church doctrine was needed. John Paul fully agreed. However, the Pope did not want to appear too heavy handed. In an address to a meeting of the Latin American bishops at Puebla in Mexico in 1979, he had tried to strike a reasonable balance. He had already publicly scolded Ernesto Cardinale during a visit to El Salvador in March 1983. Fr Cardinale was a priest, but also a minister in the Sandinista government. The Pope had given him a dressing down on the tarmac of the airport in Managua. The world's media had broadcast the Pope wagging his finger at the kneeling figure in a rare display of temper. Although the papal nuncio Archbishop Montezemolo later claimed that the Pope was urging him to regularise his position with the church in a friendly manner, the press gave a more hostile interpretation. For a Pope who rarely put a foot wrong, this was a mistake. Aware of crititicsm, John Paul did not want to do anything which would cause further discomfort. Nor, however, did he not want to do anything.

A decision was taken that, with his approval, a document would be published from the Congregation for the Doctrine of the Faith. On 6 August 1984, the Feast of the Transfiguration, the document was signed. It was a peculiar choice of timing. Italians generally take the month of August as their vacation period. So did the Vatican. By publishing it at this time, the authors expected it to get a calm launch. *The Instruction on Certain Aspects of the Theology of Liberation* was, on the whole, a balanced document. However, one of the main thrusts and purposes of the document remained clear. Salvation was a spiritual matter involving redemption from sin, not just sinful action which caused poverty. Moreover, Ratzinger emphasised that the 'overthrow by means of revolutionary violence of structures which generate violence is not *ipso facto* the beginning of a just régime'.

Pertinent to the Vatican's anxiety was also the fact that millions of people in Latin America were leaving the Catholic Church in order to join the various Pentecostalist churches. These seemed to offer a more involved form of worship. Free of any colonial past, apart from their North American sponsors, they provided a new and fresh form of Christianity.

The following year, a notification was issued from the Congregation from the Doctrine of the Faith on a book published by the great liberation theologian, Leonardo Boff. The Brazilian Franciscan friar had published a book entitled *Church: Charism and Power*. It had been delated – a term meaning 'to refer' – to the Congregation by an anonymous source. The cardinal read it. He recalled Boff well, because the friar had been his own doctoral student some years earlier. Through a mutual acquaintance, Ratzinger contacted Boff. The book contained a serious line of argument. It stated that the present hierarchy of the church was not that willed by Christ. Fr Boff, moreover, urged the church to rid itself of the structure of the ordained ministry, arguing that it was perpetuating a corrupt social structure. Boff's book was judged to be deficient and dangerous. As a theologian, he had a responsibility to teach in accordance with the tradition of the church. Anything else could only be couched in speculative terms. Boff was deeply unhappy about the way he was treated. He was asked to be silent for a year and meditate on his position, which he reluctantly did.

By now, the whole liberation theology debate had become a divisive issue in the church. Sides had been drawn up. However, a number of Latin American bishops met with the Pope during his travels and sought the opportunity to broaden his vision. Prior to his election, Karol Wojtyla's international travels had been very limited. The Communist government in Poland did not readily grant visas, even to cardinals. However, in the eight years that he had been Pope, he had travelled from New York's Fifth Avenue, where he received a ticker-tape reception, to the *favelas* of Brazil. On each trip abroad as Pope, he made sure to spend time in the *barrios*, the slums and the hovels of each country. On the one hand, he developed a broad and sure feeling for the international scene. On the other, it exposed him to the often raw violence which surrounded the people in whose midst he found himself. By 2005, Pope John Paul had made 104 pastoral visits to 129 countries, visiting over 600 cities and delivering almost 2,500 speeches. He spent over two and a half years in total outside the Vatican. In terms of distance, he had flown over 700,000 miles to all five continents. 'I could not ignore the means of modern travel,' he told a group of priests in June 2003. 'I wished to meet the men and women of our time in the everyday places where they live and work.' This brought him into contact with adoring crowds, but also with demonstrators who objected either to church teaching or to his very presence among them.

Cardinal Ratzinger rarely accompanied the pontiff on these visits. Although he was one of the Pope's closest collaborators, the cardinal took special care to remain in the Pope's shadow. He wished to avoid any misconception that he was a vice-Pope.

Pope John Paul had received some criticism for the 1984 *Instruction on Liberation Theology*, notably from Cardinal Evaristo Arns of Sao Paolo in Brazil. On 22 March 1986, a second document was issued from the Congregation for the Doctrine of the Faith. The *Instruction on Christian Freedom and Liberation* delivered more of the same message, but set an optimistic tone. The goal of theology is to help people in the search for God. The goal of liberation for people is freedom from sin, not just corrupt worldly structures.

A few months earlier, in January of that year, a number of Latin American bishops met in Peru. It was their second meeting within a year. They were deeply worried that the so-called 'liberation theologians' were tearing the church on their continent apart. Cardinal Bernard Law also attended the meeting. His presence was a reminder that the American government was viewing the developing social scene with close attention. As North America's neighbour, these countries were of particular concern. What happened in Latin America could have an immediate impact on North America. There had been rumours that Pope John Paul was going soft on liberation theology. They were anxious to relay their fears to the Vatican. The March document tried to allay their fears, as well as the Pope's desire not to cause unnecessary friction. Most importantly, the document praised the base-communities as a valid way of living the Christian life, provided the sacraments were celebrated there.

The good feelings which had been built up received a further boost the following year with the publication of an encyclical, *Sollicitudo rei socialis*. This was one of Pope John Paul's encyclicals with a deep biblical vein. Cardinal Ratzinger had been involved in the composition.

CHAPTER TEN

Other Controversies

In that same year, two theologians were to feel the weight of the Vatican's displeasure. On 25 July 1986, a letter was dispatched concerning the suspension of Father Charles Currran, who was professor of theology at the Catholic University of Washington. The American moral theologian had already run foul of the Catholic University which had censured him for his publicly taught views on sexual morality as far back as 1967. Cardinal Franjo Seper had begun to investigate his writings informally when he was Prefect for the Congretation for the Doctrine of the Faith. The Congregation examined Father Curran's writings. It found them wanting, although Father Curran protested that he had not had the opportunity of explaining them to the officials of the Congregation. The Catholic University of America took disciplinary action. Father Curran lost his job and was forced to find employment at the Southern Methodist University in Dallas.

The case brought Cardinal Ratzinger into the limelight in America. It polarised conservatives and progressives. Those sympathetic to the cardinal believed that he was the Pope's 'front man', protecting the pontiff from any backlash. Those less well-disposed began to see Cardinal Ratzinger as a heartless enforcer of the law.

These views became ever more entrenched when the Dominican Father Edward Schillebeeckx received a notification from the Congregation regarding his book, *The Church With a Human Face: A New and Expanded Theology of Ministry.* The problematic areas concerned the ordination of women and the celebration of the Eurcharist. Schillebeeckx was one of the most scholarly theologians of the twentieth century. Any move against the Belgian-born priest would have serious consequences. This time the Congregation limited itself to noting the 'deficient' character of the book. Since Schillebeeckx had already retired from teaching, the matter died down surprisingly quickly.

The reason it may have faded so rapidly was it paled in significance when a document was published two weeks later by the Congregation, entitled *Letter to the Bishops of the Catholic Church on the Pastoral Care of Homosexual Persons.* Although it was addressed to the bishops of the church, it received publicity wider than any document hitherto published under Cardinal Ratzinger's watch. Already the Congregation had published a document on the issue in 1976. The new document landed like a bombshell.

In America, some weeks earlier, the Apostolic Visitation in the Archdiocese of Seattle had come to an end. Although Archbishop Hunthausen had been informed in October 1983 that only one investigation would take place, in the event two were held. The first was led by Archbishop James Hickey, while a second was made up of Cardinal John O'Connor of New York, Cardinal Joseph Bernardin of Chicago and Archbishop John Quinn of San Francisco. As a result of the inquiries, Archbishop Hunthausen was obliged to temporarily hand over effective control of his administration to an auxiliary bishop, Donald Wuerl. In large part, the cause of difficulty was the archbishop's care for homosexual people in Seattle. The Vatican wanted a clear declaration that although homosexuality was not evil, homosexual activity was immoral and contrary to biblical evidence.

A famous riot which took place in 1969 in New York had given homosexuals greater freedom from bigotry and oppression. The Stonewall riots helped homosexual people gather under a banner of civil rights. Various 'gay rights' groups took new heart from the assault on the collective prejudice of the majority. While the document acknowledged that any kind of discrimination was wrong, it did note the biblical evidence and the tradition of the church which was clearly opposed to homosexual activity and regarded it as immoral.

The issue of sexuality was not to go away. While headway was made in several countries to ban discrimination on the basis of creed, gender, orientation, age, political views and social status, the question of sexual orientation was examined carefully by Ratzinger's team. On 23 July 1992, a document was published, *Some Considerations Concerning the Response to Legislative Proposals on Nondiscrimination of Homosexual Persons.*

In it, Joseph Ratzinger argued to legislators that it would not be unjust discrimination to take into account sexual orientation when making laws regarding 'adoption or foster care, in employment of teachers or athletic coaches and in military recruitment'. Once more there was a furore. Ratzinger calmly replied that these were real considerations which required in depth study and could not be so easily dismissed. The debate was to intensify over the coming decade. While the document decisively condemned any form of harassment or discrimination, it described homosexuality as a moral disorder.

Meanwhile, on a pastoral level, workers tried to calm the situation and heal the hurt that many homosexual people felt. For two decades a Salvatorian priest, Robert Nugent and Sister Jeannine Gramick SSND had ministered to homosexual people. Father Nugent had written extensively supporting homosexual people while Sister

Jeannine had gained support and respect for her work. All of this was to come to an abrupt end on 31 May 1999. In a curt note, the two were barred from pastoral work with homosexual people. By now, many had either drifted off or had come to an accommodation in good conscience. The purpose of the document was to clarify that the Congregation remained firm in its convictions

By the summer of 2003, the global situation had changed quite dramatically. Various groups had persuaded governments to consider same-sex unions. The Pope was strongly opposed to this development which he saw, in philosophical terms, as redefining the contract of marriage. The Congregation issued a document at the Pope's specific request. The document, *Considerations Regarding Proposals to Give Legal Recognition to Unions Between Homosexual Persons*, reaffirmed that homosexual people must be treated with equal dignity and respect, but argued that legal recognition for such unions, and the adoption of children, would ultimately be harmful for the family and society.

The theme had already been broached in 1987 with the publication by the Congregation of the *Instruction on Respect for Human Life in Its Origin and on the Dignity of Procreation*. In it the Congregation set out the church's teaching on biomedical issues such as assisted fertilisation techniques and other biomedical issues. It proved to be ahead of its time.

By now, however, the church had to deal with scandals which had emerged in a series of exposés in the media. Due to assiduous investigative journalism, various scandals had come to light involving pedophile priests in various parts of the world. In 2002, Cardinal Law was obliged to resign from the Archdiocese of Boston when his inept handling of abusing priests and victims became public. In that year, several leading American bishops were called to Rome to deal with the fall-out. Almost a year earlier, the Pope had given the Congregation the responsibility for cases regarding sexual abuse of minors by priests. The American bishops were forced into crisis meetings about the scandal which erupted following the cases which emerged in Boston and other dioceses. Cardinal Ratzinger took a lead in the Vatican's response. Although later pilloried as too little too late, seasoned Vatican observers remarked on the relative speed with which things were done. The events were by no means limited to America. Ireland, Spain, France, Brazil, Austria, Germany, England, The Philippines, Canada – from virtually every country emerged cases of abuse and inadequate responses by religious superiors.

Joseph Ratzinger never made a secret of his love of the liturgy, nor his conviction that renewal must always be accompanied by a profound understanding of the meaning of the liturgy. Just as religious belief is expressed in worship, so the liturgy helps deepen belief. It seemed therefore that the cardinal would lend a sympathetic ear to the plight of traditionalists who bemoaned the breakdown of order in the church following the Second Vatican Council.

Archbishop Marcel Lefebvre was a native of Lille. After years of working as a missionary in Africa, he was appointed Archbishop of Dakar. He attended the Second Vatican Council, where he was less than happy with the developments and the decrees which emerged from it. He was horrified in particular with the *Decree on Religious Freedom*. One of the most enthusiastic supporters at the time was the young Bavarian theologian, Joseph Ratzinger. After his retirement in Africa, Lefebvre returned to Europe. Many like-minded people were disturbed by the 'runaway church' which seemed to have lost its course. Lefebvre founded a seminary in Ecône in

Switzerland. Young men flocked to the seminary where the Tridentine Rite of Mass was celebrated and pre-Vatican II rules were maintained. Initially Lefebvre received permission to ordain priests, but by the mid-1970s, his independent actions were causing friction at the Vatican. Pope Paul VI withdrew his faculties to ordain, and suspended him *a divinis*, prohibiting him from publicly celebrating the sacraments.

Later, Pope John Paul met with Lefebvre on several occasions to try to break the impasse. Cardinal Ratzinger was very sympathetic to the French archbishop. He also loved the Latin liturgy, but he realised that it had to move on. The loss of the sacred was lamentable, but a schism was worse.

That schism came, despite desperate last minute encounters, on 30 June 1988. The final straw for Lefebvre was a meeting of world religions which Pope John Paul had arranged in Assisi in October 1986. Ratzinger privately agreed, but could not admit as much to the fiery prelate. On 30 June, Lefebvre consecrated four bishops without the papal mandate. Lefebvre and the prelates were automatically self-excommunicated. Within two days, Cardinal Ratzinger had a letter ready for the Pope to sign, offering an accommodation for all who did not wish to follow Lefebvre into schism.

The *Joint Declaration on the Doctrine of the Church*, published on 25 June 1998 was the fruit of several years of dialogue and research between Lutheran and Catholic theologians. It was presented by Cardinal Edward Cassidy, the president of the Pontifical Council for Promoting Christian Unity. Ratzinger was a keen student of Luther and had worked alongside Lutheran colleagues in universities for two decades. He greatly admired both Luther and his followers. The weak point of Lutheranism, in Ratzinger's view, is the lack of a central authority. It is this which makes Lutheranism difficult to dialogue with. The *lietmotif* of Lutheranism is the freedom which the individual enjoys on the path to salvation. Ratzinger was anxious that the Joint Declaration would not be seen in the popular mind as a total reconciliation. He therefore issued an appendix which clarified the issue. The members declared themselves perplexed. However, in early November, Ratzinger met some of the Lutherans directly connected with the declaration. The fact that he had read all the works of Luther prior to entering university impressed his Lutheran guests. The issues were ironed out, but much remained to be done. The divisions of four centuries could not be undone overnight. But for Ratzinger the role of Peter remained fundamental in any ecumenical dialogue.

Given that the Vatican has special offices which deal with Judaism and Islam, the Congregation for the Doctrine of the Faith might appear somewhat peripheral. The anti-Semitism which stained Christian-Jewish relations is one of the reprehensible aspects of Christian history. However, as Prefect of the Congregation for the Doctrine of the Faith, Cardinal Ratzinger's role was to defend and promote the Catholic Faith. Speaking at a symposium organised in Israel in 1994, he dispelled the myth that Jews were responsible for the death of Christ. Such a claim is naïve in the extreme. Only those who called for his death, and executed that call, were responsible. Nobody else could subsequently be blamed. Yet it was Pope John Paul who made the most dramatic overtures to the world of Judaism and gained the greatest amount of respect.

Similarly, Cardinal Ratzinger left the Pontifical Council for Inter-religious Dialogue to foster relations with Islam. As the fastest growing faith in Europe, Cardinal Ratzinger saw the reason in part for its expansion in the dwindling number of Christians who hold steadfast to their faith. Speaking early in 2005, he expressed his caution over the proposed entry of Turkey into an enlarged Europe. The history of both land masses is hugely different. Such an amalgamation, he believed, would require decades or more of preparation and development before it would be advisable. In a controversial publication in August, *Dominus Iesus*, the cardinal had explicitly declared the centrality of Jesus for salvation. Only churches which retain the episcopate and Eucharist may be properly called sister churches, while the goodness of world religions was recognised. Yet in his first address as Pope, Benedict XVI said that he wished to work with all religions for the 'common good of humanity'. He was careful not to claim that all were equal. To do so would be unthinkable for him and offensive to other religions. Yet, their united forces could only bring good.

Joseph Ratzinger admitted that his prefecture of the Congregation for the Doctrine of the Faith was the most difficult task he had undertaken. In the age of sound bite, the media reporting of his documents cropped the message to a few sentences. By the nature of the complex themes at issue, the message was often truncated and distorted. Nonetheless, he tried to maintain his integrity and remain faithful to his episcopal motto, to be a co-worker for the truth.

CHAPTER ELEVEN

Private Life

Rather than take up residence in the quarters provided for the Prefect, Cardinal Ratzinger chose to live in a block of apartments outside the Vatican gate. His sister Maria came to live with him, helping keep house as well as looking after his enormous private correspondence. Each summer the two would travel back to Germany where Joseph kept his house at Pentling. Here brother and sister would escape the torrid heat of Italy and entertain friends. The most regular visitor was Georg, who was delighted to see his siblings. The three would make excursions to the mountains and visit friends from their childhood.

The cardinal limited his excursions abroad to a minimum. Whatever visits he undertook were always connected to his office as Prefect. The death of his sister in 1991 came as a severe blow. He suffered deeply her loss. Friends tried to arrange for a Bavarian nun he knew from the nearby Teutonic College to help him but, in an unusual move, he invited a former music teacher, Ingrid Stampa, to move into his apartment and help him. She looked after his domestic arrangements and helped organise his personal correspondence, as well as edit some of his several books.

Joseph Ratzinger was a man of disciplined habit. He rose each morning at five o'clock. After showering and reciting his breviary, he celebrated Mass in the small chapel in his apartment. On Thursdays, he walked across St Peter's Square shortly after six-thirty when he celebrated Mass with his German co-nationals in the Teutonic College beside the basilica. After a light breakfast, he was in the office before eight o'clock. The morning was normally filled with appointments. The first two hours were dedicated to responding to pending correspondence or returning phone calls. By ten o'clock, the first audiences began. These were as varied as they were unpredictable. Bishops in Rome on their *ad limina* five yearly visits to the Vatican, theologians, foreign dignitaries, scholars, journalists, pilgrims, ex-students, representatives of other Christian denominations or world religions all called to see him. The list was endless. By midday these usually ended, allowing him to return to work. As a member of several other Vatican Congregations and committees, there was preparatory work to be done and interminable meetings to attend. He left the office most days at one-thirty, and walked across St Peter's Square, carrying his briefcase. A few curious tourists would salute him, guessing he must be important. He returned their greetings with a nod and a smile.

After lunch, usually taken at home, he took a short nap before going for a walk in the neighbourhood. He preferred to walk alone. Less than an hour later, he was back at desk work, either in his apartment or in his office. This brought him up to dinner, before which he recited evening prayers in the chapel. The round of liturgies and ceremonial events he had to attend often disrupted the pattern of his day.

When time permitted he spent Saturday evening and Sunday as a day of rest in the hills outside Rome. His briefcase usually accompanied him even there.

It is also important to note his extraordianary literary output. Some of his published books are listed on page 96. When he asked Pope John Paul if accepting the prefecture of the Congregation would mean an end to his writing career, the Pope replied that he remained an individual, and therefore could publish as an individual. Ratzinger did so. Although he had no time to publish the deep scholarly works he wished to, he did compose a number of popular works. He shrewdly realised that the vast majority of people no longer read heavy tomes. Rather he chose the more colloquial style which he found matched what he had to say. Early in 1985 he published an interview with the Italian journalist, Vittorio Messori, called *The Ratzinger Report*. It took a rather jaundiced view of several of the developments in church life since the Second Vatican Council. In October of that year, the extraordinary Synod of 1985 was held to mark the twentieth anniversary of the ending of the Second Vatican Council. Several of the bishops were heartened by the frankness of Ratzinger's book-length interview. They were emboldened to make wide-ranging criticisms of the last two decades. The *Final Declaration* admitted as much. Cardinal Bernard Law noted that doctrine seemed on the retreat, observing that people no longer knew the fundamentals of their faith.

The following year, Pope John Paul decided to act on this observation. He commissioned a twelve-member committee, under the presidency of Cardinal Ratzinger, to prepare a new catechism. The cardinal chose a young Austrian Dominican, Christopher Schönborn to act as Secretary-General. The working language chosen was French, a detail noted by the Italians who saw their hegemony being threatened. The catechism was not structured on the traditional formula, *question and answer*. Rather it was divided into four parts. These dealt with the Apostles' Creed, the Sacraments, the Ten Commandments and Christian Prayer. After six years of intensive labour, the work was ready. Pope John Paul signed the first copy on the thirtieth anniversary of the opening of the Second Vatican Council.

When he reached his 75th birthday in 2002, Joseph Ratzinger submitted his resignation to Pope John Paul. The pontiff asked him to remain at his post a little longer. A year later, he reminded the Pope of his age, hinting that he would like to retire to Bavaria to write. But by now Karol Wojtlya was severely incapacitated by Parkinson's Disease. 'How could I leave the side of the Pope?' he later asked, accepting the renewal of his mandate.

CHAPTER TWELVE

The Election

The death of Pope John Paul on 2 April 2005 was not unexpected. Already by early January it was clear the Pope was gravely ill. Although speculation on a successor is forbidden, people wondered who would succeed the Polish Pope. While some argued that it would be impossible to choose an Italian, or even a European, others saw Joseph as the most obvious candidate. His name began to circulate among the cardinal-electors. At 77 – he turned 78 on 16 April – he would not be likely to have as long a pontificate as John Paul II. He above all cardinals had the greatest amount of theological preparation and experience. If short, his pontificate would nonetheless continue the work of Pope John Paul. The Pope and Prefect had met each Friday evening to discuss the issues arising at the Congregation. The conversation was always in German. The Pope often invited Cardinal Ratzinger to lunch on Tuesdays, where the two men, alone or with guests, would chat about plans for the future of the church.

The morning of the conclave, 18 April, Cardinal Joseph Ratzinger led the cardinals in the Concelebration of the Mass for the Election of the Roman Pontiff. The Mass was celebrated at the High Altar of St Peter's. The basilica was crammed to capacity. Thousands crowded to see a spectacle which they had not witnessed for over twenty-five years. The world's cameras were trained on the diminutive figures of the cardinals as they processed towards the centre of the church. Speaking under the cupola of Michaelangelo, Cardinal Ratzinger delivered a meditation on what type of person he judged the cardinals must choose. Although he would not likely have searched for the position, he must surely have realised that he stood a strong chance of emerging as the new pontiff.

Standing where Pope John Paul had delivered his homilies for more than quarter of a century, Joseph Ratzinger painted a pen picture of the world:

How many winds of doctrine have we known in recent decades, how many ideological currents, how many ways of thinking? The small boat of the thought of many Christians has often been tossed about by these waves – flung from one extreme to another: from Marxism to liberalism, even to libertinism; from collectivism to radical individualism; from atheism to a vague religious mysticism; from agnosticism to syncretism and so forth. Every day new sects spring up, and what St Paul says about human deception and the trickery that strives to entice people into error (cf Eph 4:14) comes true.

Today, having a clear faith based on the Creed of the church is often labelled as fundamentalism. Whereas relativism, that is, letting oneself be 'tossed here and there, carried about by every wind of doctrine', seems the only attitude that can cope with modern times. We are building a dictatorship of relativism that does not recognise anything as definitive and whose ultimate goal consists solely of one's own ego and desires.

We, however, have a different measure: the Son of God, the true man. He is the measure of true humanism. An 'adult' faith is not a faith that follows the trends of fashion and the latest novelty; a mature adult faith is deeply rooted in friendship with Christ. It is this friendship that opens us up to all that is good and gives us a criterion by which to distinguish the true from the false, and deceit from truth.'

In a few lines, he succinctly displayed the perennial weakness of so many novelties of the modern world. There is a deep hunger for spirituality, he acknowledged. Today's generation, however, is often confused as to where that may be found. Christians also find themselves buffeted from side to side as the small boat on a stormy sea. But their fidelity to the 'different measure' would see them through their difficulties. The clarity of his thought struck many.

That afternoon 115 cardinals from 52 countries entered the conclave. They cast their ballots before Michaelangelo's great fresco of the Last Judgement in the Sistine Chapel. The next afternoon, on the fourth ballot, Joseph Ratzinger exceeded the required 77 votes, or two thirds majority. Asked to accept and take a name, he chose the name Benedict in honour of Giacomo della Chiesa, who had been Pope Benedict XV (1914-22) during the First World War. It was also a tribute to St Benedict, the fifth-century founder of Western Monasticism.

The votes were burned and white smoke billowed from the chimney above the Sistine Chapel. The crowds which gathered in St Peter's Square below squinted into the pale grey sky. Slowly the great bells of the basilica began to toll. A new Pope had been elected! The bells rang throughout the city, alerting the Romans that they had a new bishop.

The cardinals had chosen continuity. The Pope was led to the Room of Tears beside the Sistine Chapel. Here the papal tailor was waiting. Exchanging his red soutane for the white robes and red mozzetta, he returned to the altar to receive the obeisance of the cardinals.

By now the piazza was full. Word had spread like wild-fire. Throughout the world, television and radio pro-grammes flashed the news from Rome. A new Pope had been chosen. There was electrical tension as the crowds waited for the Cardinal Proto-Dean to make the official public announcement. He greeted the crowd in several languages before the ancient words, *Annuntio vobis gaudium magnum*. 'I announce to you a great joy.' *Habemus papam*. 'We have a Pope.' When he called out the name Joseph Ratzinger, there was a silence, before he informed them that the new Pope would be called Benedict XVI. There was a roar of excitement. He was the first Teutonic Pope in almost a thousand years. The last Germanic Pope was the Swabian, Victor II (1055-57.)

Several minutes passed before the new Pope appeared on the balcony. Lifting his hands in a gesture of salute, the new Pope addressed the crowd: 'Dear Brothers and Sisters! After the great Pope John Paul II, the cardinals have elected me, a simple and humble worker in the Lord's vineyard. I am consoled by the fact that the Lord knows how to work even with insuffient instruments and above all I commend myself to your prayers and ask your support.' Having given the Apostolic Blessing to the city and the world in Latin *(Urbi et Orbi)*, the Pope waved once more and withdrew. His life had now changed utterly.

Reaction was immediate. There was general surprise at Ratzinger's elevation. He was by no means an unknown candidate. His name stirred up strong emo-tions. Even those who knew little or nothing about him found they had strong opinions about Joseph Ratzinger. The Pontificate of Benedict XVI would certainly not be neutral or passive.

CHAPTER THIRTEEN

The Pontificate

A humble worker in the vineyard of the Lord
The morning following his election, the Pope appeared at breakfast in the guesthouse where the cardinals had remained. Congratulating the pontiff, Cardinal Schönborn, the Austrian cardinal, commented that he looked well in his new white robes. 'I will need time to get used to them,' Pope Benedict retorted jovially.

But already time was passing. He had spent the early evening writing a speech to be delivered at the end of Mass which he celebrated in the Sistine Chapel at 9.00 that morning. In it he laid out some important themes for his pontificate.

'My sole concern is to proclaim the living presence of Christ to the whole world.' For this he recognised the need for bishops and the Bishop of Rome to work in close harmony, a clear reference to collegiality. He also pledged to work for the implementation of the Second Vatican Council, which ended forty years ago this year.

'Theological dialogue is necessary,' he continued, 'the investigation of the historical reasons for the decisions made in the past is also indispensable.' He promised to do everything in his power to promote the fundamental cause of ecumenism.

After the Mass, the 78-year-old pontiff paid a call to his former colleagues at the Congregation for the Doctrine of the Faith. It was a relaxed affair, but there was no mistaking the joy and affection as the Pope entered the building. After a short address, Pope Benedict greeted the staff individually. He had spent almost a quarter of a century in the position as Prefect and it was a very human gesture to return. Knowing of his sweet tooth, one of the staff had bought a cake which was presented to him before he left.

The same morning, the Pope took possession of his apartments on the top floor of the Apostolic Palace. Vatican observers were surprised to see his personal assistant, Ingrid Stampa walking three steps behind him.

Naturally, the papal apartments needed a coat of paint. The new Pope chose to stay in the Domus Santa Marta where he was lodged during the conclave which elected him. However, in a surprise move, the Pope visited his old apartment beside the Colonnade of St Peter's on Thursday and Friday afternoons. He spent three hours there each day, writing his homily for the Inaugural Mass and looking over pending appointments in the Roman Curia. In a temporary move, he reconfirmed all the positions formerly held by curia members until he had time to consider new candidates. A large crowd gathered at the Vatican entrance of Sant' Anna to see the Pope come and go. On Saturday, his books and personal items were transferred to the Papal Apartments where decorating had already begun.

That same morning the Pope met with journalists at the Paul VI Audience Hall. In a brief address in Italian, German, French and English, the Pope thanked the media for the extraordinary coverage of Pope John Paul's demise, his funeral and the subsequent conclave. The audience lasted less than twenty minutes but several journalists were pleased with the Teutonic punctuality and the fact that it ended so promptly. That afternoon he returned to his apartment, now almost empty, to sit and chat with his brother who had arrived from Regensberg.

On a magnificent April morning, Pope Benedict XVI

celebrated Mass as the 265th pontiff since St Peter. The Mass of the Inauguration was a splendid celebration. Despite forecasts of rain, the morning dawned with a light breeze, a photographer's delight. Some 400,000 people crammed into St Peter's Square along with dignitaries from all over the world. Shortly after 9.30 am, the Pope vested for Mass and went to pray at the tomb of St Peter underneath the High Altar of the basilica. Here the *pallium* and *Ring of the Fisherman* had been left overnight. They were removed from the niche above the tomb and carried in the procession which made its way through the main doors of Carlo Maderno's great façade of St Peter's. When the Pope made his entrance, there was a loud burst of applause. Vested in a gold chasuble and mitre, he paused briefly to salute the throng. As the Litany of the Saints gave way to the entrance antiphon, the crowd took up the chant 'Benedetto! Benedetto!'

The Mass was celebrated in Latin. In a gesture to his predecessor, he wore vestments which had been used by Pope John Paul II. After the gospel was sung in Latin and Greek, the Pope was given the *pallium* and ring to mark the beginning of his Petrine ministry.

This was the first time that a new rite of installation had been used since the Second Vatican Council. In former years, the pontificate publicly began with the coronation with the papal tiara. The *pallium* is a strip of white wool which is draped across the shoulders of archbishops, a sign that they are spiritual shepherds. The *pallium* which Pope Benedict was given was modelled on one dating back to the fourth century. The long band of white wool was embroidered with five red crosses to symbolise the wounds of Christ on the cross. *The Fisherman's Ring* is a large gold seal with the image of Peter casting his net. In former times, documents were sealed with it.

In his homily, Pope Benedict continued to indicate the

lines along which his pontificate would run. He would be both a shepherd and a fisherman, looking after those entrusted to his care and casting a net of friendship to 'those of other cultures'. The new Pope was interrupted by applause thirty-three times, especially on the occasions he mentioned Pope John Paul II.

At the end of Mass, Pope Benedict mounted the popemobile made famous his predecessor and drove through the crowds. He received a great welcome, especially from the hordes of Bavarians who had made the trip.

For Pope Benedict, the morning was not over. After he had unvested and took his place on a throne in front of the High Altar. Here he received the dignitaries who lined up to offer their good wishes at the beginning of his pontificate. He was remarkably relaxed and indeed looked as if the papacy was nothing new to him.

On Monday evening he travelled to the basilica of St Paul-outside-the-Walls, to honour the mortal remains of Paul, teacher of the Gentiles. It was a fitting beginning to the pontificate of a former professor of theology now charged with communicating the Christian message in the twenty-first century. That theme he took up once more when he visited St John Lateran, the cathedral of Rome. Here, on the site where the first Christian basilica was built by Constantine in the early fifth century, Pope Benedict observed that the *cathedra*, or chair, is the seat of teaching authority. 'This may frighten many within and without the church. They wonder if it is not a threat to freedom of conscience, if it is not opposed to freedom of thought. However, the Pope does not teach of his own accord. Rather he remains faithful to the tradition developed since Christ lived on earth, that Christ who continues to live in the Christian community.'

When he met with diplomats accredited to the Holy See on 11 May, the new Pope emphasised his awareness of contemporary history. He acknowledged that, as a German, he had a particular appreciation for those involved in war, as he himself had lived through the horrors of the Second World War. 'For my part, I come from a country in which peace and fraternity have a great place in the heart of its inhabitants, in particular, of those who, like me, knew war and the separation of brothers belonging to the same nation, because of devastating and inhuman ideologies that, cloaked in dreams and illusion, imposed on human beings the yoke of oppression. You will understand therefore that I am particularly sensitive to dialogue among all people, to overcome all forms of conflict and tension, and to make our world a world of peace and fraternity. Uniting efforts, all together, the Christian communities, leaders of nations, diplomats, and all people of goodwill, are called to realise a peaceful society to overcome the temptation of the clash between cultures, ethnic groups, and different worlds. To achieve this, every nation must draw from its spiritual and cultural heritage the best values of which it is bearer, to go out without fear to meet the other, ready to share its spiritual and material riches for the common good.' He stretched out a hand of friendship to many nations which had sent representatives to the funeral of Pope John Paul II, inviting them to establish diplomatic relations. The Pope may have had in mind such countries as China, Vietnam and Saudi Arabia. The last is the home of many shrines sacred to Muslims, notably Mecca. Under the previous pontificate the number of countries seeking accreditation had quadrupled. Benedict's invitation was a clear overture to further linking the world's nations and the world's religions, to work for the common good of humanity.

When he met the Israeli ambassador, Oded Ben Hur, the Pope took him by surprise. As the ambassador went to greet him at the end of the audience, Pope Benedict said, 'I have good news for you. I will visit the synagogue in Cologne when I attend the World Youth Day in August.' Pope John Paul II was the first Pope to visit a synagogue when he went to the synagogue of Rome in 1986.The Jewish community of Cologne is the oldest of Germany. Its origins date back to the 4th century. Now a German Pope would visit a synagogue where his fellow country men had tried to annihilate the Jews in the Holocaust. This would be a momentous day indeed.

A further surprise was in store. On 13 May, the Pope met with the clergy of Rome. During the encounter, he announced that he had dispensed with the five-year rule to begin the beatification process for Pope John Paul II. Normally five years had to elapse from the death of a person until a formal investigation had taken place to verify that person was a worthy candidate for beatification.

The first visit outside Rome would be to Bari, in the south east of Italy on 29 May. It was an ideal venue, an Italian city which was to host the International Eucharist Congress, during the Year of the Eucharist. It would please the Italians and focus the church on the 'summit and source' of its spiritual life.

With the appointment of the 68-year old William Levada, Archbishop of San Francisco, as the new Prefect for the Congregation of the Doctrine of the Faith, Benedict began his rearrangement of the Roman Curia. His choice of the American, whom he had known while Levada worked in the Congregation between 1976-82 was something of a surprise. The widely tipped Cardinals Christoph Schönborn of Vienna and Tarcisio Bertone of Genoa may have been too obviously European. The selection of Levada for Pope Benedict's key position was seen as a vote of confidence in the American church which was struggling after the exposé of child abuse. Further appointments in the Roman Curia would come piece-meal as the positions became vacant. Having worked in the environment for almost twenty- five years, Benedict would be in no hurry.

The initial public reaction, which had been in places hostile, gradually began to change. Media headlines calling him God,s Rotweiler, or the Panzar Cardinal seemed to have been somewhat exaggerated. His erstwhile colleague, Hans Küng, who had often been critical of Joseph Ratzinger the theologian, graciously called for the public to grant him ˡa hundred days of grace.‰ Even those who had little interest in him prior to his election as leader of the world,s 1.3 billion Catholics discovered their need to inform themselves about the life and thought of Joseph Ratzinger, Pope Benedict XVI. The reserved Bavarian, who had hoped to spend his life in academia, had been catapulted onto the world,s stage at the age of 78. Every word was analyzed, each gesture was reported. The first pontificate of the third millennium had begun.

A Selected Bibliography of
Joseph Ratzinger

The Meaning of Christian Brotherhood (Ignatius Press, 1993, original in German 1960)

Theological Highlights of Vatican II (Paulist Deus Books, 1966)

Introduction to Christianity (Seabury Press, 1979, original in German 1968)

The Ratzinger Report: An Exclusive Interview on the State of the Church (Ignatius Press, 1985)

Behold the Pierced One: An Approach to Spiritual Christology (Ignatius Press, 1986)

Principles of Catholic Theology: Building Stones for a Fundamental Theology (Ignatius Press, 1987)

The Church, Ecumeniosm and Politics: New Essays on Ecclesiology (Crossroad Publishing Company, 1988)

The Nature and Mission of Theology: Essays to Orient Theology in Today's Debates (Ignatius Press, 1995)

Called to Communion: Understanding the Church Today (Ignatius Press, 1996)

Gospel, Catechesis, Catechism: Sidelights on the Catechism of the Catholic Church (Ignatius Press, 1997)

A New Song for the Lord: Faith in Christ and Liturgy Today (Crossroad Publishing Company, 1997)

Salt of the Earth: The Church at the End of the Millennium (Ignatius Press, 1997)

Milestones: Memoirs 1927-1977 (Ignatius Press, 1998)

Many Religions – One Covenant: Israel, the Church and the World (Ignatius Press, 1999)